100 WALKS IN
East Sussex

compiled by

P. L. O'SHEA

AND

B.M. O'SHEA

(plus Goldie & Ash, their *constant* companions)

The Crowood Press

First published in 1994 by
The Crowood Press Ltd
Ramsbury
Marlborough
Wiltshire SN8 2HR

British Library Cataloguing-in-Publication Data
A catalogue record for this book is
available from the British Library

ISBN 1 85223 807 0

All maps by Janet Powell

Typeset by Carreg Limited, Ross-on-Wye, Herefordshire

Printed in Great Britain by Redwood Books, Trowbridge, Wiltshire

CONTENTS

PUBLISHER'S NOTE

We very much hope that you enjoy the routes presented in this book, which has been compiled with the aim of allowing you to explore the area in the best possible way – on foot.

We strongly recommend that you take the relevant map for the area, and for this reason we list the appropriate Ordnance Survey maps for each route. Whilst the details and descriptions given for each walk were accurate at time of writing, the countryside is constantly changing, and a map will be essential if, for any reason, you are unable to follow the given route. It is good practice to carry a map and use it so that you are always aware of your exact location.

We cannot be held responsible if some of the details in the route descriptions are found to be inaccurate, but should be grateful if walkers would advise us of any major alterations. Please note that whenever you are walking in the countryside you are on somebody else's land, and we must stress that you should *always* keep to established rights of way, and *never* cross fences, hedges or other boundaries unless there is a clear crossing point.

Remember the country code:

Enjoy the country and respect its life and work
Guard against all risk of fire
Fasten all gates
Keep dogs under close control
Keep to public footpaths across all farmland
Use gates and stiles to cross field boundaries
Leave all livestock, machinery and crops alone
Take your litter home
Help to keep all water clean
Protect wildlife, plants and trees
Make no unnecessary noise

The walks are listed by length – from approximately 3 to 12 miles – but the amount of time taken will depend on the fitness of the walkers and the time spent exploring any points of interest along the way. All the walks are circular and most offer recommendations for refreshments.

Good walking.

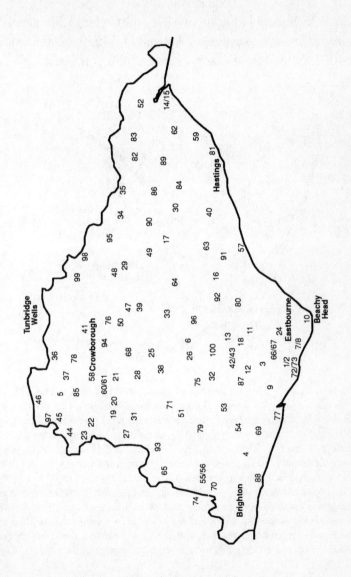

Walk 1 HINDLEAP WARREN 2¹/₂m (4km)

Maps: OS Sheets Landranger 187; Pathfinders 1248 and 1247.
A good short walk, sometimes wet and including an uphill stretch.
At 402326, the 'Goat' car park, west of Wych Cross.

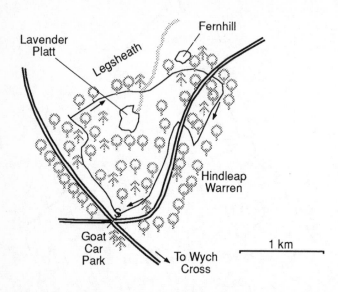

Leave the car park in this quiet part of **Ashdown Forest** by a narrow track which leads into woods to meet a bridleway indicated by a horse-head sign. At a junction, with a track going right, into Lavender Platt, go across, maintaining direction through a birch plantation. Turn right at a path T-junction, descending to reach another junction in rather more open land. Turn left there, and after about 70 yards, turn right, downhill through the heather. Stay on this new track, ignoring cross-rides, to reach a wet area and a stream. Cross the stream, turn left (the ground here is still boggy at times) and, ignoring footpaths left and right, continue to reach a quiet road. Go straight across and continue uphill to reach a crossing bridleway. Turn right and climb up to reach extensive views across the Forest and the Weald. The route is now heading south-westerly towards **Hindleap Warren** with its ditch and bank: continue with this on the left, turning right after 300 yards on to a rough track and following it down to reach the road again. Cross the road once more, go through a clearing (an old car park) and then turn left, uphill, on a path that keeps parallel to the road. After 400 yards the path forks: take the right fork which leads back to the 'Goat' car park.

POINTS OF INTEREST:

Ashdown Forest– The forest is mainly open heathland and is an ideal walking area with over 80 miles of wide bridleways and 'rides' as well as many narrower footpaths through fields, heather, gorse, pines and deciduous trees. Fallow deer, badgers, grass snakes and, occasionally, adders are not uncommon companions for walkers. The Forest Centre, near Wych Cross (Grid ref: 432323), is a 'must' for visitors.

In this north-western district Ashdown Forest is less often visited and, in consequence, is much quieter. The trees are mainly ash, elder, sycamore and birch, but yews and oaks are also seen. The heathland tends to be invaded by birch, pine and rhododendron hereabouts. There are also some Scots pine, identified by their orange bark and grey-green needles arranged in pairs.

Please take special care in all parts of Ashdown Forest – carelessness results all too often in heath and woodland fires with expensive damage and loss of wild life. Fire beaters are stored and available in all car parks but seek help from the Rangers if necessary. Please take your litter home, but leave the wild plants and flowers.

Hindleap Warren – The boundary ditch and bank are what remain of the rabbit farms of three hundred years ago.

REFRESHMENTS:

Definitely bring your own!

Walk 2 SHEFFIELD FOREST, PARK AND GARDENS 2¹/₂m (4km)

Maps: O S Sheets Landranger 198; Pathfinder 1269.

A stroll through woodlands with millpond, wild flowers, maybe deer and certainly ducks and swans.

Start: At 410259, Furner's Green, between North Chailey and Danehill, off the A275.

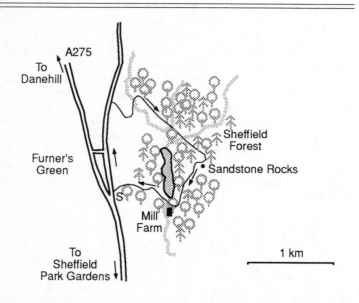

Park off the main road and walk north along the side road which runs almost parallel to it. Go past the village, staying with the road as it winds towards Tanyard Farm. Look out for a stone marker to the right: there, follow a deep and wooded track as it descends to a footbridge. Cross and climb up, forking right to reach a clearing. Now go along a field edge and make for the middle of the wood ahead to reach a clear path into **Sheffield Forest**.

Cross a ditch and continue along a narrow path as it ascends to the hilltop. At a cross-track, turn right and descend to cross a stream. Now follow the path a short distance to reach another junction. (A short diversion left, here, leads to some oddly

10

shaped sandstone rocks). There is a millpond over to the right at this point, and by continuing southwards along the path you will arrive at a watermill. Turn right there to go across the millpond dam. It is now a simple matter to return to the start: merely follow the lane up and westwards from the mill, to return to Furner's Green.

POINTS OF INTEREST:
Sheffield Forest – A gentle stroll through the headwaters of the Sussex Ouse in this wooded area of East Sussex, especially in Spring or Autumn, is a delightful curtain-raiser to a visit to the famous Sheffield Park Gardens. The mill-wheel still exists, minus its paddles. Flour was ground here until the 1930's. Four hundred years before that, cannon were cast here – is this why the lane to Furner's Green is so sunken – heavy iron dragged by oxen?

Sheffield Park Gardens lie to the south of the route. They are open in spring and summer through to October. A visit is a 'must' – superb colours, specimen trees, cascades, waterfalls, five lakes, azaleas. Autumn is especially spectacular. And no funfair or blaring music! Check the opening times by telephoning 0825 790231.

REFRESHMENTS:
There is a tearoom in Sheffield Park Gardens.
There are also refreshments in the nearby villages of Danehill, Newick and North Chailey.

Walk 3   THE AIRMAN'S GRAVE   3m (5km)

Maps: OS Sheets Landranger 198; Pathfinder 1269

A short walk, on southern slopes, to a reminder of World War II.

Start: At 456289, the car park, $1^1/_2$ miles north-east of Nutley.

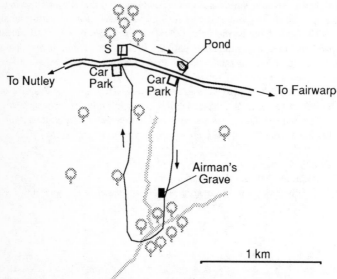

From the car park, walk through the pole barrier towards the clump of trees on the far side of the open area. On reaching the trees, turn right along a wide track, going downhill to reach another car park. Continue for a further 300 yards to reach the man-made Ellison's Pond. Go round this to reach a road, and cross it to reach a third car park (The Hollies). Leave this car park half-left (i.e. south-easterly) on a clear wide path. Soon, the path turns southerly and descends through **heather**. After almost a mile (about $1^1/_2$ kms) of walking towards a dip in a wooded valley you will reach a small sandstone enclosure. This is the **Airman's Grave**. The route continues by maintaining direction, going downhill towards the stream among the trees. This section of the route is often muddy. Turn right over the second stream and after a further 100 yards turn right again, going uphill on a grassy bank. The bank leads back to the road reaching it close to two car parks, the further one of which was the starting point for the walk.

POINTS OF INTEREST:

Heather – Ashdown Forest (*see* Note to Walk 14) has many fine areas of colourful heather – common ling, bell heather and cross-leaved heath. Newts abound in the ponds, fallow deer can often be seen, especially at dawn and dusk and lizards bask in the sun. Indeed there is much to interest the naturalist on this route or the marked forest walks.

Airman's Grave – It is not a grave, of course, but a memorial to the young pilot and crew of a World War II Wellington bomber. Returning from a raid over Europe the bomber crashed here in the forest – perhaps attempting to land on the airfield near Wych Cross. The pilot's mother originally marked the spot with flowers and a simple wooden cross, and the Forest Rangers, the Conservators, the local Riding Association and the Air Training Corps continue the upkeep. Wreaths are placed in the local stone enclosure and the spot is visited by many people every week.

REFRESHMENTS:

None, en route, but available at Nutley ($1\frac{1}{2}$ miles south-west).
The King William IV, Nutley.

Walk 4   **BECKLEY'S WOODLANDS**   3m (5km)

Maps: OS Sheets Landranger 199; Pathfinder 1271.

A short and easy woodland walk, superb in Spring or Autumn.

Start: At 862243, Beckley crossroads on the A268.

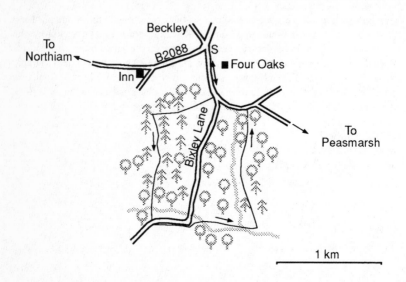

Begin by walking south from the **Beckley** crossroads (the junction of the A268 and the B2088) for 300 yards and, as the road swings left towards Peasmarsh and Rye, note the lane ahead, Bixley Lane, but take the stile by the footpath sign to the right. The path leads westwards, with woodland to the right. Keep diagonally left along the fence on your left, going to the rear of a house and barn. Go through a gap into a conifer plantation and after about $^1/_2$ mile, as the woods end, turn left (southwards) descending along the edge of Bixley Wood for about $^3/_4$ mile. The trees are a rare mixture of hornbeam, pine, and chestnuts, and bluebells are profuse in season.

   Go under power lines and over a stream, then through a gate and into a lane. Turn left for about 400 yards (heading eastwards) going under more power lines. Go over a stream by way of a wooden bridge to reach a track crossroads. Here turn left along the rough track heading northwards, keeping generally to the fence on your left.

14

Go under power lines yet again and ascend through oaks and chestnuts as well as beech trees. Woodland walking now brings you to the main road by way of a gate. Turn left to the Bixley Lane junction and follow the road round the right-hand bend to return to the start.

POINTS OF INTEREST:

Try tree-spotting while enjoying this walk – chestnut, oak, silver birch, Scots pine, Douglas fir and hornbeam are all here. There is also a fine collection of woodland flowers, which should be left for others to enjoy too.

Beckley – The village is referred to in King Alfred the Great's will as it was an important centre of the Sussex Iron industry. All Saints Church has an 11th century spire and a 15th century east window, fascinating, grotesque corbels and a dug-out chest, banded with iron, to keep ecclesiastical treasures in.

There is an attractive children's farm on A268 nearby – Great Knelle Farm – which includes a blacksmith's forge, tractor-drawn train, farm animals and a 'talking scarecrow'. (Tel: 0797 26321).

REFRESHMENTS:

The Rose and Crown Inn, Beckley is $^1/_2$ mile west of the start.

Walk 5   FOREST ROW AND BRAMBLETYE   4m (6½km)

Maps: OS Sheets Landranger 188; Pathfinder 1248.

A short and pleasant farmland walk west of Forest Row, passing a Jacobean ruin.

Start: At 425351, The Square, Forest Row.

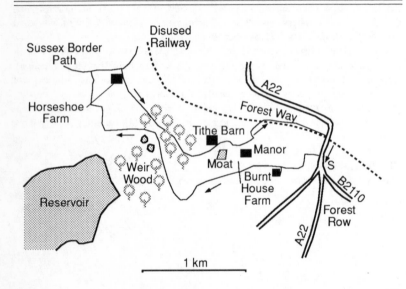

From The Square, take the path beside the National Westminster Bank to reach a footbridge. Cross and bear half-left through a caravan park to reach a gate. Go through and around the field beyond with the hedge on your right. On reaching a stile, go over and continue to reach a gate. Go through on to a track leading to Burnt House Farm. Cross the track to reach a stile near a barn. Go over and walk to a gate just past the barn. Go through and turn right to follow a lane into a field, then bear half-left to the far corner. On reaching a stream keep to the left bank and follow it to a lane. Go straight over (<u>not</u> over the bridges) and through a gate. Go down the middle of a field to reach another gate and bridge. Cross this bridge, then go half-left along the path leading to Weirwood Reservoir.

When the path reaches a tarmac lane, turn right to reach the reservoir gate. Cross the stile to the right, then go straight on to reach another stile and a footbridge. Go over and continue along the boundary wire to reach a third stile. Beyond this the fence curves left (westward) until a woodland area is seen ahead. Now follow a signpost pointing right and then go across two fields with stiles to reach a footbridge. Go over and turn right – you are now on to the Sussex Border Path. Go along the right field edge to reach a T-junction of paths and two bridges. Go over the larger bridge and continue to the entrance of Horseshoe Farm. Turn right through a gate and then go straight on to a gate and stile. Keep around the left edge of the field beyond, and cross a stile in the corner. Go right, but very soon left on a raised path into a copse. On emerging from the trees, keep ahead, going to the left of a tithe barn, and on to **Brambletye Manor House**, passing the 'castle', to the right. Now follow a lane turning north to reach an old level-crossing and a cottage. Go past the cottage, then turn right, immediately going through a gate and on to Forest Way, a disused railway line. Follow the Way to the A22 and turn right along it to return to **Forest Row** and the start of the walk.

POINTS OF INTEREST:

Brambletye Manor House – The house is the ruin of a Jacobean manor or castle, complete with moat. Built in 1631, the house still has one of its four-storey towers.

Forest Row – The village is an ideal start for many walks to the north of Ashdown Forest. There are cafés and pubs and, with care, good parking spaces. In the grounds of the Health Centre is an oriental plane tree planted from a seed of the tree reputed to have sheltered Hippocrates (of medical oath fame) on the Greek Island of Kos, when he lectured to his pupils. The tree appears to be very healthy.

REFRESHMENTS:

The Forester's Arms, Forest Row.

There are also other opportunities in Forest Row.

Walk 6   GUN HILL AND CHIDDINGLY   4m (6½km)

Maps: OS Sheets Landranger 199; Pathfinder 1289.

A short but varied walk through farmland and woods.

Start: At 565145, the Gun Inn, north of Eastbourne.

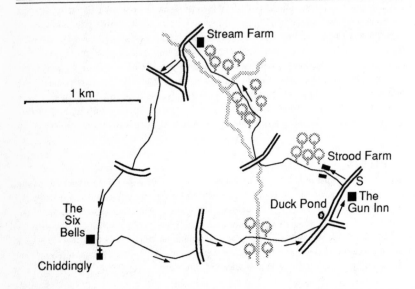

Go through the imposing gated entrance to Strood Farm, a few yards north of The Gun. Go past the farmhouse, on the left, and downhill between buildings to reach a wooded area. Keep the wood on the right and descend to a lane at Bull Bridge. Go straight over on to a track through a field. The track climbs a little to the right, but it is best to keep fairly near the stream, to the left, towards the bottom left corner of the field, and then to turn half-right. Climb up, keeping watch for a gap in the hedge which appears before the top of the field is reached. Go through and across the next field, making for another hedge-gap slightly lower down and near a corner. It can be a little difficult to locate this gap, so take care. Beyond, the walk enters a delightful wood with bluebells and other woodland flowers at the appropriate season. Ignore crossing paths, keeping ahead along a narrow path to reach a bridge over a noisy stream. Now ascend to Stream Farm, to the right, and go between converted buildings to reach a lane. Turn left, downhill. As the lane starts to climb again, and to curve left, look out for a gate on the right with a 'Wet Land' warning sign. Go through, and heed the warning by keeping up and left of the marshy patch, to reach a stile. Go over and keep left to emerge through a thicket into a field. Go up the field, with a hedge on your right, to the top right-hand corner.

At this point care is needed. It is necessary to descend to the lane ahead, but the stile in the hedge a yard or two to the right could be in need of repair! On reaching the lane, go right through a gate and cross a field towards another field corner where a fence can be seen running from right to left. You are now heading directly for a tall church spire about a mile ahead: this is the next objective. At the fence corner (where there is a reassuring yellow arrow pointing the way) keep straight on, going through or over squeeze stiles and gates to pass a riding school, to the left, to reach a lane. Turn right for ten yards or so to reach a gate, on the left. Go through, and up the field to reach another gate in a hedge. Walk alongside the right-hand field hedge, going through two stiles in quick succession to reach a narrow hedged path. This leads clearly to the church and post office at **Chiddingly**. Turn left, passing a car park, to the left, to reach the church, noting a Domesday plaque en route on the right wall.

Just past the end of the car park go over a stile on the left, and walk to a stile and gate by keeping close to the hedge on the right. Continue along the right-hand edge of the next field to reach a lane, some cottages and a fine oast conversion. Follow the lane past a farmhouse with a low flint wall curving left, and then go up to a crossing lane. Turn left, going uphill to pass 'Scrapers'. Cross a stile in the hedge on the right, marked with a Wealdway sign, and follow a downhill path to meet a 'Ramblers' bridge over a stream. Cross the bridge and follow the track half-left to a little wood. Go through the wood and straight on across a field. Now go slightly left to reach a rickety stile. Cross gingerly and walk across the next field, making for an oast which appears to be in the far field corner. Cross a stile on to a lane. Turn left, pausing to admire the duck pond to the left, but ignoring the lane signposted for Cogger's Cross, to return to The Gun.

POINTS OF INTEREST:
Chiddingly – The village church boasts a 128 foot high stone steeple and a splendid monument to Elizabeth I's Baron of Exchequer, Sir John Jefferay, in alabaster.

REFRESHMENTS:
The Gun Inn, at the start.
The Six Bells, Chiddingly

Walk 7   **A Short Walk near Battle**   4m (6½km)
Maps: OS Sheets Landranger 199; Pathfinder 1290.
Field paths and forest walk. In fact, a short easy stroll.
Start: At 725184, near Netherfield Village.

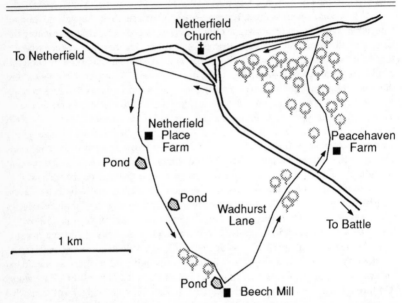

Park just to the south of the church at **Netherfield,** at a Y-junction of roads. Go over a stile by a green box head westwards across the scrubby area. Just before reaching the road to Netherfield, turn left to head southwards. Now, when a sunken track is reached, go left and almost immediately right, over a stile and along the right side of the field beyond. A further 20 yards brings you to a gate. Do not go through: instead, turn back into the field and make for the far left corner to reach a driveway. Follow the drive to Netherfield Place Farm. Turn left by the big building and go across the concrete to reach a grassy path. Follow this as it curves right and goes through a gate.

Continue in the same general direction by the trees to the right, going along the right edge of two fields to reach a gate. Go through and bear gently left across the next field, going downhill to the bottom left corner where there is a pond. Cross a muddy dam into the next field (beyond a gate with iron steps). Now make for the stile ahead and go over it into a wooded area. After a short distance ignore the crossing path, continuing ahead through a patch of conifer trees, walking beside a fence. By the pond on the right, there is a stile in front of Beech Mill: go over and turn left, between banks, along a clear path (Wadhurst Lane). After about 100 yards keep straight – do <u>not</u> go right – go uphill and between high banks for about $^1/_2$ mile (800 metres) to reach the Battle road. Turn right for a further 100 yards, then go left through a gate by a bungalow. After about 200 yards, turn left and go across a field and down to a stream. Cross two stiles into the forest ahead, through which a narrow path descends to cross another stream by a plank bridge. Cross another stile and then across another footbridge across a second stream and go forward to reach a crossing path. Take the path to the right and walk through the wood to reach a lane. Turn left along the lane to reach a road junction near the church. Here turn left to reach the start of the walk.

POINTS OF INTEREST:
Netherfield – The church is dedicated to St John the Baptist. Inside there is an oil painting of his head on a platter – very gruesome!

REFRESHMENTS:
No refreshments en route, but at Battle, about two miles south-east, there are plenty of opportunities.

Maps: OS Sheets Landranger 198; Pathfinder 1289.
Gentle, flat and lush walk with birdsong and a Tudor Manor.
Start: At 502132, the Roebuck Inn, on the B2124, Laughton.

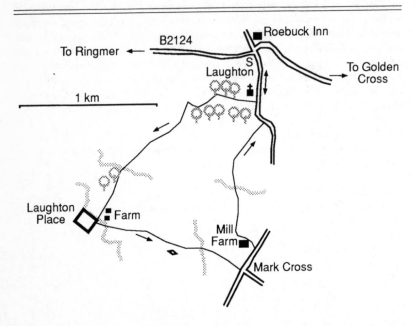

Cross the main road and walk south along the lane opposite which leads to the church. Turn right into the churchyard of **All Saints, Laughton**. Walk through and, at the rear, take the footpath leading due west through a long and narrow wood, usually full of birdsong. At the wood's end, go over a stile and turn half-left, walking across to a gate. Go through and turn right, then left, so that you are walking along a field with a hedge to the left. Now go diagonally across a field along another field with a hedge to the right and down to a footbridge over a stream.

Cross the bridge and go over the first stile on the right and cross the next field to reach another bridge. Cross and go straight over the next field, to reach a stile. Go over and then through a metal gate. The tower of **Laughton Place** is now ahead: make for the path between the farm buildings. Turn left opposite a bridge (you are now heading east) and walk to the top left field corner. Go straight on through three gates to reach a pond to the right. Now go over a stile and walk past a ruined barn, to the left, to reach a gate. Go through, then go over two more stiles to reach a road at Mark Cross.

Turn left along the road for 250 yards, then go left into Mill Farm. The track keeps right, going around the farm and then ahead, along the left side of a field. Turn right in the next field and head for Laughton Church. Go through a gate and a gap, then over two streams to reach a field with buildings off to the right. At the far end of this field you emerge on to a road just before a bridge. Turn left along the road to return to the start.

POINTS OF INTEREST:

All Saints, Laughton – Parts of the church date from 1229 and much is 14th century. Inside, there are helmets dated 1540 and 1660, a bible from 1717, a musicians gallery dated 1821 and a tablet recording local people killed by a flying bomb during World War II.

Laughton Place – This was probably the first brick-built Tudor residence, though little remains of the original. The stone bridge was once a drawbridge. Demolition and renovations have proceeded over many years and the site now has tenants again. The Tower is 51 feet high and has metre-thick walls at the base.

REFRESHMENTS:
The Roebuck Inn, Laughton.

Walks 9 & 10 KING'S STANDING AND NUTLEY WINDMILL 4m (6½m) or 7m (11km)

Maps: OS Sheets Landranger 188; Pathfinders 1269 and 1243.
Two walks in Ashdown Forest, using rides and tracks.
Start: At 473302, King's Standing car park, at the junction of the B2026 and the B2188.

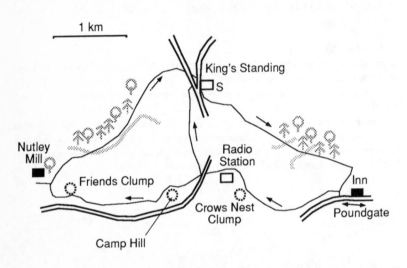

Although in **Ashdown Forest** these walks are almost entirely across open heathland where a compass might assist, though prominent clumps of trees help in decent visibility.

Leave the car park heading eastwards, aiming just to the right of a mound. Now follow a bridlepath (signed with a nag's head!) that wanders south-easterly and downhill towards the forest boundary. Go across two streams, then climb up for about ½ mile (¾ kms) to reach another track on the right. Take this to reach a busy road. Turn left for a cautious 200 yards to reach the Crow and Gate Inn if refreshments are required. If you are not visiting the inn, turn right before reaching the road and make for Crow's Nest Clump, westward across the valley. When a fork is reached, keep right of a barrier, and head for the right side of the Clump. Once past it, keep the radio station on your left and continue to reach the B2026. Cross the road with care.

The shorter walk, turns right 20 yards after crossing the road, heading due north along the **Wealdway**. Walk past several car parks, to the right, and superb views, to the left, to reach a Y-junction of roads. The start is just across the junction.

For the longer walk: after crossing the B2026 near a small car park ('Roman Road'), head south-westwards and uphill, making for 'Camp Hill' (which is more than 600 feet above sea level and topped by a Clump). About 400 yards of walking will bring you to a point to the right of the Clump. The path now heads westwards and somewhat downhill towards another Clump and two ponds. Bear a little right by the right-hand pond and walk parallel with a road to the left, climbing towards Friends Clump. When you are just to the left of the Clump, go forward for about 200 yards to reach a narrow path signposted to **Nutley Windmill**. To visit the mill go through a gate on the left. To continue with the walk, go right, cross a stile and walk through bracken to reach a bridlepath. Turn right, but after another 50 yards, go left and downhill. Now ignore crossing tracks and make for the woodland, going gently downhill and heading north-easterly. Go past Old Lodge Bottom to reach a stream. Cross the stream and continue along the valley floor, with heathland to the right and trees to the left. The path now leads uphill, and eventually passes a little waterfall (The Garden of Eden!). Continue towards the B2026, but turn right just short of the road in order to regain at the start.

POINTS OF INTEREST:
Ashdown Forest– The forest is mainly open heathland and is an ideal walking area with over 80 miles of wide bridleways and 'rides' as well as many narrower footpaths through fields, heather, gorse, pines and deciduous trees. Fallow deer, badgers, grass snakes and, occasionally, adders are not uncommon companions for walkers. The Forest Centre, near Wych Cross (Grid ref: 432323), is a 'must' for visitors.

The Wealdway – This excellent long distance footpath begins at Eastbourne and runs 80 miles to Gravesend.

Nutley Windmill – The windmill is a small, and probably very old, wooden construction that has been restored and sometimes operates. It is open on some Sundays in the summer months. Tel: 0825 712632 for information.

REFRESHMENTS:
The Crow and Gate Inn, Poundgate.

Walk 11   ISFIELD   4m (6½km)

Maps: OS Sheets Landranger 198; Pathfinder 1289.

A gentle stroll with time to explore Isfield. This could combine with walk 76 to make an all-day 11 mile route.

Start: At 450174, the telephone exchange, Isfield.

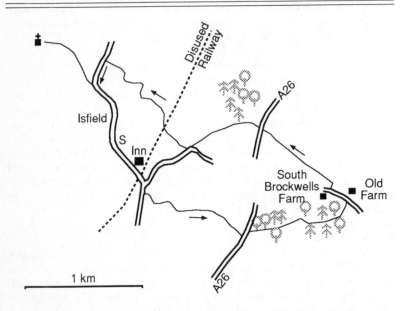

Begin by walking south-east through **Isfield** village, noting the Singing Fish Inn, to the left, and the restored railway station. Beyond the level crossing, turn right towards Lewes and look for a concrete way marker by a gate to the left, less than a hundred yards from the crossing. Take this drive, bearing right in it, passing buildings to the right. Go over a stile by a gate to the left and walk with the hedge on your left. Go through the gate ahead and turn right, along a fence, to reach the trees ahead. Continue through the wood and then cross two fields to reach Brook Lodge Farm. The footpath goes right, through the farm, and then bears left to reach the busy A26. Turn left along the road but, after 35 yards, cross with great care to enter a little wood through a gate. Walk beside a railing on a bank, go over a wire fence and maintain direction eastwards with the wood on the left. Cross a stile, go through a gate and walk into the wood on the clear track to the left. When the track peters out some 200 yards further on, go left for about 25 yards to reach a stile in a wire fence. Cross and cut across the field beyond to reach a gate on to a lane at Old Farm.

Turn left along the lane for 200 yards. On reaching South Brockwells Farm, to the left, go right (due north) through a gate. Walk along the left hedge in the field beyond, turning left when it ends to walk to the field corner. Cross a ditch and a stile and walk to a gate. Go through and continue to meet a hedge coming in from the right. Keep ahead, walking alongside this hedge – it is on your right – to reach the A26. Again cross with caution and go through the gate ahead. Walk alongside the hedge on the right to reach a stile in the field corner. Cross and bear left a little, still with the hedge on the right, to pass through a gate. Maintain the same direction across the next field and go through another gate on to a lane. Immediately go right by a signpost, going through a gate and crossing a field with a fence to the left to reach another gate. Now cross a disused railway line running north-south. Go over a bridge and turn right between fences. Go through the gate at the end of the fences and turn left. After about 300 yards go through a gate to reach a track and follow it for 250 yards to reach a stile into a garden. Keeping the poultry sheds on the right and a large pit on the left cross to reach the village lane in Isfield. Turn left to return to the starting point.

POINTS OF INTEREST:
Isfield – The Uckfield-Lewes railway line was a victim of Mr Beeching's axe in the 60's. It is now known as the Lavender Line. The village station has been lovingly restored and is enhanced by steam engines and coaches from former times.

A short detour across the fields from the village leads to St Margaret's Church with its collection of Shurley tombs. There is said to be an underground passage from the church to nearby Isfield Place where the Shurleys resided.

REFRESHMENTS:
The Singing Fish Inn, Isfield. The inn was once a chapel!

Walk 12   FOREST ROW AND PIXTON   4m (6½km)

Maps: OS Sheets Landranger 188; Pathfinder 1248.

Footpaths north of Forest Row with fine views north and south.

Start: At 426352, the Forester's Arms, Forest Row.

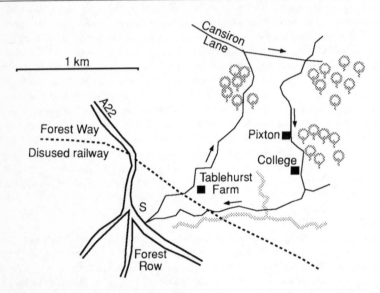

Take the path opposite the Forester's Arms and follow it to the village green. Turn left, and then go to the right of the timber yard. Turn left, cross a footbridge and go through a kissing-gate to reach the Forest Way (a disused railway line). Now take the footpath to the right, following it between fences, behind the Scouts' HQ and on to the drive leading to Tablehurst Farm. At the farm, keep left on a concrete road, following it into a field. Turn left and walk to a stile. Go over and continue to another stile. Go over and forward into an area of woodland. Go straight through, reaching a clearing with power lines overhead and there turn right to reach a pylon. The path beyond narrows, and then widens to reach a barbed wire fence with a stile to the left. Cross and turn right to maintain direction as you go alongside bushes, to the left, to reach another stile. Go over and forward into **Cansiron Lane**.

Turn right along the lane and look out for a stile, to the right, near Saxon's Mead. Cross and go half-right across the field ahead, following the waymark arrows to reach a hedge. Go under the power-lines again, with Highams Wood on the left. On arriving at crossing paths, take the left-hand path, with a hedge to the left, and go down towards Pixton Hill Farm. The track becomes metalled, with college buildings to the right and woodland to the left and, later, on both sides. At the next path junction, turn right and descend the shoulder of the hill to reach a stream. Follow the path, with the stream to the left, passing Tablehurst Farm now on the right, and continuing to meet the Forest Way track. Go through the gate ahead and go in front of the Scouts' HQ. Now follow Station Road into **Forest Row** to return to the start of the walk.

POINTS OF INTEREST:

Cansiron Lane – The lane is a fine view point, if visibility permits. Southwards, beyond Forest Row, is Ashdown Forest. Hartfield is eastwards, while to the north is Dry Hill and Hammerwood, with the Greensand Ridge further away.

Forest Row – The village is an ideal start for many walks to the north of Ashdown Forest. There are cafés and pubs and, with care, good parking spaces. In the grounds of the Health Centre is an oriental plane tree planted from a seed of the tree reputed to have sheltered Hippocrates (of medical oath fame) on the Greek Island of Kos, when he lectured to his pupils. The tree appears to be very healthy.

REFRESHMENTS:

The Forester's Arms, Forest Row.

There are also other possibilities in Forest Row.

Walk 13   HARTFIELD TO AN ENCHANTED PLACE $4\frac{1}{2}$m (7km)

Maps: OS Sheets Landranger 188; Pathfinder 1248.

A short walk in Ashdown Forest.

Start: At 477357, parking carefully in Hartfield.

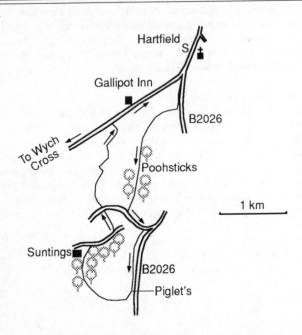

Take the road south, going out of **Hartfield** towards Wych Cross. At the fork take the B2026, left, for about 600 yards, then turn right on to a public footpath. Follow this over a stile, then bear left to go over two more stiles into a valley. On coming to a road, bear left on to a bridleway which leads to a wooden bridge. (Those who know their A. A. Milne will be happy to know they are now on the very bridge where 'Poohsticks' was invented). Continue on the footpath beyond, going through woodland to reach a road. Turn left and proceed to a junction. Here turn left (eastward) for about 100 yards and then take the wide bridleway by a line of tree-stumps to the right. The bridleway runs parallel with the B2026 for about a mile ($1\frac{1}{2}$kms), passing the car parks of 'Wrens Warren' and 'Piglets'. You are now at the top of the forest with excellent views all around. At the 'Piglets' car park turn right and look out for a circle of trees at a path junction. This is The Enchanted Place, another fine view point.

Continue westward and take the next bridleway going right (north- westward) and downhill. Ignore two bridleways, to the right, but on reaching a fork take the right-hand branching, going down to reach a road. Turn right along the road, passing 'The Rough', right, and 'Suntings', left. Go straight on at the next junction and continue downhill to reach White House Farm. Immediately past the farm, to the left, go through the farmyard and over a brick stile in the right-hand corner, in front of a garage. Cross the field ahead, go over a stile and now make for the opposite corner of the next field to emerge on to a private road. In front of a concrete barn, take the second left turning, then bear right and climb the stile beside a gate. Turn right and follow the path on the left. Carry on to a footbridge, cross and go ahead to reach a stile in the top right of the next field. Go over and walk round the left edge of a field to reach the top corner. Go over a stile and follow a path as it leads round to the left. At the 'Hartfield' sign turn right, cross a field to its top corner and go over a stile. Now head for the opposite corner and go over another stile. Now go through the wood to reach a stile. Go over and cross the top of the next field. Go over another stile on to a lane. Turn left and on arriving at the Forest Row – Hartfield road turn right. Walk past the Gallipot Inn, and follow the road, bearing left along the B2026, back to Hartfield.

POINTS OF INTEREST:

Hartfield – This attractive 15th century church has an unusual lych gate adjacent to a cottage, as well as the 'Pooh Corner' shop full of A. A. Milne memorabilia.

Ashdown Forest – Today the forest is more 'open heathland with trees', and offers views of the North and South Downs. The Vanguard Way and Wealdway long distance paths cross it and there is a very informative Visitor Centre, with displays, guidebooks and specimens, near Wych Cross, at Grid Reference 432323.

Walkers familiar with the books for children by A. A. Milne will be especially attracted to the local part of the Forest, where Piglet, Eeyore and Pooh Bear's other friends had their adventures.

REFRESHMENTS:

The Gallipot Inn and also other opportunities in Hartfield.

31

Walk 14 FORD'S GREEN AND CHELWOOD CORNER 4¹/₂m (7km)

Maps: OS Sheets Landranger 198; Pathfinder 1269.

A walk in Ashdown Forest, with heath and farm land and some fine views.

Start: At 444273, the sport's field opposite the King William IV Inn, Ford's Green.

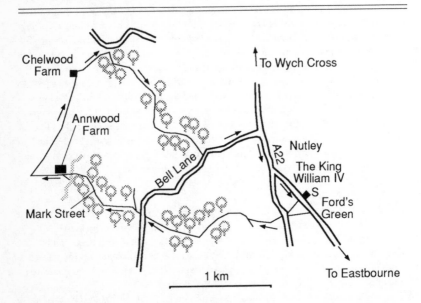

Keep to the right of the sport's field changing rooms and go westward to reach a lane. Cross and go right to reach a track, with a signpost, leading to Prickets Hatch. Ignore crossing drives to arrive in a farmyard, and take the grassy bank off to the right (with a hedge on its right side), following it into a wood (part of **Ashdown Forest**). Follow the woodland path as it descends. Ignore a broad crossing track and, as the path narrows and clears, curve round to the right to reach a footbridge over a stream. Go over and continue to a meeting point of footpaths on a sandy track. The route now follows a westerly direction: cross the track and bear right for a few yards right before turning left and uphill on a narrower path. Now look for a metal gate – there are riding stables to the right and yellow arrow waymarkers. Follow the arrows round the fence and a training ground and paddock to reach a road (Bell Lane). Cross and follow the sign to Mark Street Cottage. Now follow a sandy path into the wood on the left and, when the path divides, take the centre one to reach a yellow arrow pointing the way, left and downhill. At a crossing track where there is a pond on the right, go across, following the path beside the pond, then bearing down to the left. Now go uphill (using steps) to reach a field to the left of Annwood Farm.

Go up to the top right-hand corner of the field and cross a stile. Keeping a hedge on the right, go across the next field but, half way across, by a telephone pole, turn right into the right-hand corner where there is another stile. Go over and walk along a fenced lane to reach Chelwood Farm. Walk through the farmyard, continuing for another 500 yards to almost reach the Chelwood Corner road. The route now swings away to the right, as indicated by the yellow arrow on a telephone pole. Cross a wide track, then bear left to enter a wood. Follow the yellow marked trees, going downhill. In the distance you should now see some tall pine trees: make for these, eventually emerging into the open. At the pine trees, keep left to reach a gate. Go along the edge of the next field and, on meeting a fence, ignore a lane heading left. Maintain the same general direction, southerly, with a fence to the left, until you are alongside a wood, also on the left. Now look for a signed stile leading into the wood. Cross the stile, skirt round a pond and descend on a path heading south-easterly between banks. Cross a footbridge, then go uphill and bear left to reach a lane. Go left, following the lane to reach a main road (the A22) at Nutley. Go right along the edge of the A22, taking great care, to return to the start of the walk.

POINTS OF INTEREST:

Ashdown Forest– The forest is mainly open heathland and is an ideal walking area with over 80 miles of wide bridleways and 'rides' as well as many narrower footpaths through fields, heather, gorse, pines and deciduous trees. Fallow deer, badgers, grass snakes and, occasionally, adders are not uncommon companions for walkers. The Forest Centre, near Wych Cross (Grid ref: 432323), is a 'must' for visitors.

REFRESHMENTS:
The King William IV, Ford's Green.

Walk 15　　　**SOUTH OF BURWASH**　　　$4^1/_2$m (7km)

Maps: OS Sheets Landranger 199; Pathfinder 1270.

Kipling landscape, Burwash village and, perhaps, a visit to Bateman's?

Start: At 675247, Burwash village car park.

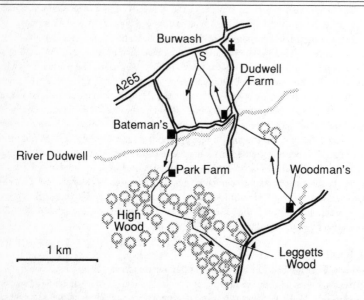

Leave the **Burwash** car park at the back, left corner to reach a narrow path going downhill with hedge to the right. Go over the first of many stiles, cross the field beyond and another, continuing with a hedge to the right. Cross a stile in a hedge and descend across a field to reach a lane. Turn right and follow the lane until you are facing **Bateman's**. Now turn left and walk through Park Farm. When you are opposite the last barn on the right, go left through a gate. Turn right beyond the gate and go uphill with woods to the right. At the top, enter High Wood through a gate. Walk ahead to reach a clearing and there turn left on to a track descending in an easterly direction. Ignore a cross-track to keep going down on what is now a narrow path to reach a stream. Cross the stream and go steeply up, curving right, then left. The path narrows, but after 250 yards it joins a wider path coming in from the right. Follow the new path to reach a lane by a sign for Leggetts Wood.

Turn left along the lane for 400 yards, then bear right on a lane signed for Etchingham. Turn left down steps just past 'Woodman's, and cross a field to reach a gate. Go through and across the next field. Now, go down towards the corner of a wood and at the bottom corner cross a stile into the wood. Shortly, go over a ditch, then go left across a rough area to reach a stile. Go over into a field corner. Now cross the long field, heading for Burwash Church spire ahead. At the far left corner go over another stile, and descend to cross the fence by steps and go up along the right side of the field beyond. At the next corner go into another field, leaving the fence to the left to meet another fence on the right. Go over a stile in this fence and descend, on a path that soon runs between banks to reach a drive. Follow the drive to a lane.

Turn right along the lane. Cross a river and then take a lane to the left, towards Dudwell Farm. Go past the farm and turn right through a gap in a hedge near some railings. Walk forward to reach a stile. Go over and continue with a hedge on the right. Go over a footbridge and a stile and then left, uphill, following the field edge to the left. After about 250 yards go over a stile on the left and along the woodland track beyond. Go over one more stile into a field corner and walk along the left hedge to meet the outward path and the car park.

POINTS OF INTEREST:

Burwash - Walkers should not miss the ceramic footpath map displayed in the village street, the work of a local artist. There are also many fine, well-preserved cottages, a Norman church at the eastern end of the village and a red-brick house, Rampyndene, with an ornately carved porch of flowers, cherubs and strange birds.

Bateman's – Rudyard Kipling lived here from 1902 until 1936, but the house was built in 1634 by a local ironmaster. The author's study, and his 1928 Rolls-Royce, are as he left them. The house is owned by the National Trust and is open from Good Friday until the end of October. Tel: 0435 882302.

REFRESHMENTS:

A good selection in Burwash.
There is a tea room and a picnic site at Bateman's.

Walk 16   **MAYFIELD AND MOAT MILL**   4¹/₂m (7km)

Maps: OS Sheets Landranger 199; Pathfinder 1269.

A short walk requiring careful navigation, but including an
attractive village.

Start: At 587268, the car park south of the High Street, Mayfield.

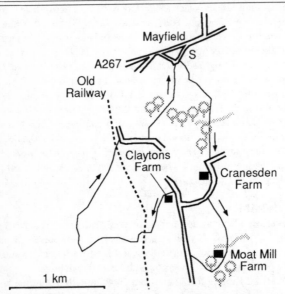

Leave the entrance of **Mayfield's** car park, turn right and right again, and at the next junction turn left – it is a public right of way! At the end go through a gate and drop down past allotments to reach a wood and a brook. Continue southwards through the wood and on emerging, walk along two fields, going first along the right side then along the left, but not going back into the wood. Continue to reach a lane and go forward along it, going down to a little brook and then up away from it. Go past Cranesden Farm, on your right, then look for a stile to the left, as the lane veers right. Cross and take a path along the right edges of several stiled fields to reach a footbridge. Cross and go on to reach a gate. Go through and on to reach a little wicket gate where there is a wall on the right. Go through and after 10 yards or so, go right into Moat Mill Farm, passing a converted oast, to the right, to reach an access drive. At the next junction, turn right, cross a bridge and go right over a stile. Go diagonally across the field beyond to reach another stile, going over on to a lane.

Turn right along the lane, ignoring a right turn, and following it for about $^1/_2$ mile ($^3/_4$kms).

About 200 yards after the lane turns left, go sharp left along the access drive to Clayton's Farm. Continue beyond the farm, eventually bearing right and going under an old railway line. Turn left beyond the line and then, in the next field, turn right, with a hedge and a brook to the right. In the field beyond, go over on to a short stretch of path and follow it into a field corner. Maintain direction for 500 yards, with the brook on your right, then go over a footbridge. Now head northwards, with a hedge and trees to the right, to reach the next field corner. Cross a concrete road and go through the gate opposite. Walk to a second gate and go through to descend, with a hedge on your right. Go over a stream, through some trees and up alongside field edges to reach the buildings of Knowle Farm. Go over the old railway and into a lane. Turn right and after 350 yards turn left on to a grass path. After 50 yards fork left – do not take the more obvious, wider track, to the right – and go between several large trees. Now go left, through a gate and into a field. Turn right and after 20 yards go over railings to find a stile behind a brick building in the corner of the field. Cross and climb the steps ahead to reach another stile. Go over and descend into the wood below. Maintain direction, going over a stream and up to a lane. Turn left, but soon go right between houses to reach the starting point.

POINTS OF INTEREST:

Mayfield – Find time to explore this ancient Wealden village, which has been called 'the sweetest village in England'. Study the village sign (in High Street) and note the Old Palace next to the church, where Archbishops of Canterbury once lived. Just inside the gate of the United Reformed Church is a stone commemorating Protestant Martyrs burned to death here in Tudor times.

REFRESHMENTS:
The Rose and Crown Inn, Mayfield.
The Carpenters Arms, Mayfield.

Walk 17 **HERSTMONCEUX CASTLE AND OBSERVATORY** 5m (8km)
Maps: OS Sheets Landranger 199; Pathfinder 1290.
A moated castle and the 'Greenwich' observatory.
Start: At 643103, near Herstmonceux Church.

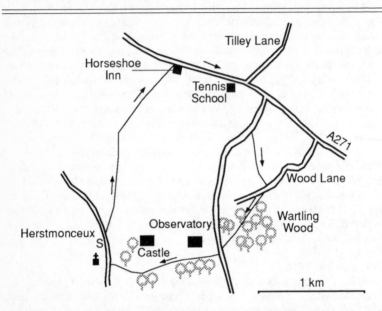

Walk back towards the main A271 road, that is, in a northerly direction, and opposite
a house on the left, about 250 yards from the church, take the signed bridleway along
a woodland track. Go through a gate and continue the edge of a wood. **Herstmonceux
Castle** can now be glimpsed, off to the right. Now descend across a field to meet
another path in the valley. Keeping on the clear path go through another gate and then
climb up, with a fence to the left, to reach yet another gate, with some trees on the
right. Keep the fence on the right, continuing in the same direction as the track becomes
rather sunken. On reaching a stile, go over and follow the lane beyond to reach the
A271 at the Horseshoe Inn.

    The village of **Herstmonceux** is a mile away to the left here. The local area is
called Windmill Hill after the tall black windmill to the left. Turn right along the main
road, crossing with care to reach the safety of the pavement. Continue eastward, passing

in front of a Tennis School, looking out for Tilley Lane coming in from the left. At this point go back across the main road to reach a stile and signpost just beyond the School's boundary. Cross the stile and bear left, going along the left edge of a field to reach a stile. Go over, cross the road beyond and go through a gate to the right of Lawn Cottage. Go ahead down the hill to reach a little stream, crossing it on a plank bridge and walking on to reach a stile. Cross the next field and go up to the left end of a barn at Wood Lane. Cross to a stile in the hedge opposite and go right into Wartling Wood. Follow the path through the wood, with a fence to the left, going straight over at a cross-paths to reach a small clearing. Maintain the same direction through more woodland ahead, passing a pond to the right, and continuing to reach a tarmac road (Wartling Road) close to the castle gate. Keeping a wooden fence to the right, go directly ahead through a gate to pass the Telescope Buildings, on the right. Go over a track and across grassland to reach a large dead tree. Pass to the left of the tree, with the Castle to your right and then go slightly right between some trees. Go through several gates, over a road and a farm track to emerge on a lane just below the church where the walk began.

POINTS OF INTEREST:

Herstmonceux Castle – Moated and built of warm red bricks, this splendid castle was built in the middle of the 15th century, dismantled in 1777, but restored in the 1930s. When, in 1948, the smoke and grime of London restricted good astronomic conditions at Greenwich, the Royal Observatory moved here. Recently even sunny Sussex has become too polluted and the work of the observatory has moved again, this time to the clearer air of the Canary Islands.

Herstmonceux – The village is the centre of Sussex trug-making – the oval-shaped baskets of split willow and chestnut so useful to gardeners and shoppers. When they were displayed at the Great Exhibition of 1851 Queen Victoria was so impressed with them that the local craftsmen delivered several to her, walking to London and back to provide the service.

REFRESHMENTS:

The Horseshoe Inn, Windmill Hill.
There are also several good pubs in Herstmonceux.

Walk 18   ARLINGTON AND ABBOT'S WOOD   5m (8km)

Maps: OS Sheets Landranger 199; Pathfinder 1308.
Field paths and a fine woodland walk.
Start: At 544075, Arlington village car park.

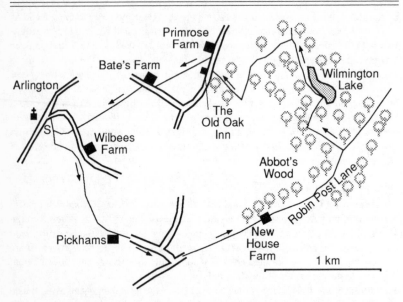

Take the little enclosed path opposite the Yew Tree Inn, going south-eastwards to
reach a gate. Go through and continue straight ahead to reach another gate to the right
of some trees. Go through again and turn left alongside the edge of the field beyond.
At the corner, cross the concrete road which leads to Wilbees Farm, and go half-right
across the field ahead. Walk in a more southerly direction and look for a gap in the
fence. Go through (not over the stile to the left) and head for the corner of the field
directly ahead, maintaining direction to reach a stile. Go over, turn right and, very
soon, go left on to a tree-lined track which is sometimes overgrown and muddy. The
track leads to 'Pickhams', on the right. Keep ahead, passing 'Hayread' to reach a lane
on the left. Ignore this, continuing for another 150 yards to reach a junction. Turn left,
passing Old Thornwell, to the left. You are now on Robin Post Lane: follow for

almost 1¹/₄ miles (2kms). At first, the lane is firm underfoot, but it deteriorates, becoming rough and often muddy as it enters **Abbot's Wood**.

Pass New House Farm, ignoring a crossing track about 300 yards beyond. After another 600 yards, turn left along a wide track opposite a Forestry Commission notice. After a further 400 yards there is a notice informing you that you are on a Forest Walk: turn right and follow the waymarks down to the Wilmington Lake. Follow the posts with the water on the right, passing a weir and continuing with a stream over to the right. About 300 yards past the weir, turn left and slightly uphill for ¹/₂ mile (800 metres), ignoring a broad crossing track. Walk in a southerly direction and, at the next crossways, take the right-hand path to emerge from the wood on to a lane. The Old Oak Inn is across the road.

Go right, up the road, to reach Primrose Farm. Turn left into the farm entrance, then go left again between the buildings. Go over a stile beside a gate and walk past a line of trees to the left. At a field corner, turn left over a double stile across two fences into a further corner. Keep on, with trees on the right, going alongside fences towards the farm buildings ahead. You will soon reach a lane close to Bates Green Farm (which has a splendid 'Bluebell Walk' at the appropriate season, and where turkeys are reared). Turn right along the lane, passing the farm entrance and then, shortly after, go left through a gate. Before another gate, go right, then left, to walk along the left edge of two fields. In the corner of the second field, go straight on, through a gate and across the field aiming beyond, to pass to the right of a pylon. Continue to a stile on to a lane. Cross to the path opposite, following it alongside a garden and into a field. Aim half-right towards the church spire to reach a gate on to the path used to leave Arlington. Turn right to retrace the route the short way back to the start.

POINTS OF INTEREST:
Abbot's Wood – The wood is managed by the Forestry Commission but was once owned by the monks of Battle Abbey. Wilmington Lake was a fishpond for the Abbey.

REFRESHMENTS:
The Yew Tree, Arlington.
The Old Oak Inn, on the route.

Walk 19   **WYCH CROSS AND BRABERRY HATCH**   5m (8km)
Maps: OS Sheets Landranger 187; Pathfinders 1248 and 1269.
A gentle walk through mixed woodland and heath.
Start: At 419315, near Wych Cross on the A275.

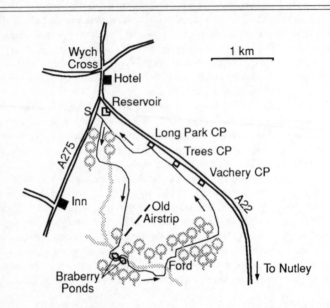

About 400 yards south of Wych Cross, on the A275, there is a car park near a reservoir. This is the starting point. Look out for the **Old Toll Charges** on the old Lewes road before setting off.

Go past the pole barrier to the right, and then straight ahead, walking parallel with the A275. Go gently downhill and southerly, and on reaching a junction, after 400 yards take the left fork. Walk a further 400 yards to approach a fenced field. Just before reaching the fence, turn left (the fence will now be on your right) and go over a sleeper bridge and up a track across open country. Follow the track to a junction of many pathways. Turn right, southerly, and go steadily downhill to reach a T-junction. Turn left here to visit an old World War II **Emergency Landing Strip**.

The walk does not turn left, however, but continues southerly into woodland, soon reaching the ponds at Braberry. Cross the stream, then turn left between the ponds. Cross the stream again by going over the dam, and then walk easterly, keeping the stream on your left. After about 800 yards, cross the stream again at a ford and bridge. Now ascend gently through woodland along a clearly defined path with fences both sides, one fence soon replaced by the high wall of a training college. The path curves left and approaches the busy A22: keep left and walk parallel to the road, going alongside the Trees and Long Park car parks. Shortly after passing these, go left (south westerly) for 250 yards, then turn right to walk back to the Reservoir car park.

POINTS OF INTEREST:
Old Toll Charges – The A275 is the old road to Lewes and a Toll House was situated here, on the green at the junction between the A275 and A22. You can still see a brick base (once part of the Toll House wall) on which the charges are set out. Nowadays the car park is free!

Emergency Landing Strip – Perhaps the Wellington crew who died at the Airman's Grave (*see* Note to Walk 3) were making for this emergency strip, now over fifty years old but still clearly defined. The soil, Ashdown sand, has lost its top layer of humus and plants have great difficulty in growing.

REFRESHMENTS:
None en route but available in Chelwood Gate and at the *King William IV*, Nutley.

HOLTYE ROUNDABOUT 5m (8km)

Maps: OS Sheets Landranger 188; Pathfinder 1248.

Farmland paths, fine views, some woodland, quiet lanes and a small stretch of Roman Road.

Start: At 462392, the White Horse Inn, Holtye.

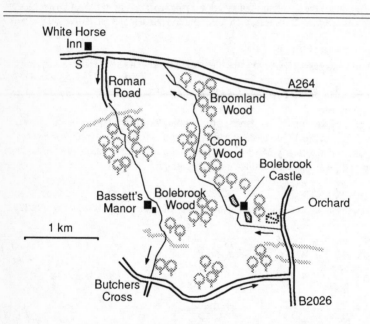

Walk east from the inn, going along the A264, with care, for about 250 yards to reach a gate on the right. Go through and take the track beyond, the course of a **Roman Road.** The track descends past a fenced section maintained by the County's Archeological Trust, and then heads southwards, going over a bridge in the right-hand field corner. Now ascend along the hedge on the left, and at the top turn left and then right, using a path through woodland. Go out of the wood at a fingerpost, and follow it across a field to reach a pylon in the far corner. Go over a stile on to a track and turn right, and immediately left, and then right again, on to a clear track. Follow the track to a gate. Go through and continue to Bassett's Manor. After pausing hereabouts to admire the view, continue southwards through the farm's buildings, going downhill to reach a stream. Cross and walk for 400 yards (passing a wooded area to the left) to reach a quiet lane running left and right, at Butcher's Cross.

Turn left along the lane, following it for a mile (1^1/$_2$kms), gently downhill and round bends to reach the B2026. Turn left for 500 yards and then take a clear track on the left. Walk with an orchard to the right, then continue to reach a field corner. Turn right beside lakes, then go left and very shortly right, to walk close to Bolebrook Woods and the ruin of Bolebrook Castle, to the right.

For the next mile (1^1/$_2$kms) the route is north-easterly and north. At first the path is clear, with a stream and rising ground to the right. The way then narrows into Coomb Wood. When the path forks, keep right and continue, going by a pond to the left. Now go under the pylon lines and along the left side of a field to reach the next field corner, by another pond beside Broomland Wood. Go half-left across the next field to reach the A264. Turn left along it, walking with care, to return to the start.

POINTS OF INTEREST:
Roman Road, Holtye – This is a well-preserved section of road, the line of which, southwards, can be followed on the Pathfinder sheets 1248 and 1269 as it crosses the Hartfield road near the Gallipot Inn, a little east of Wrens Warren camp and Camp Hill. The road ran from Lewes to London and was probably used to carry corn from the South Downs and Wealden iron to Londinium and the channel ports. A hundred yard section of the road was excavated in 1930, the excavation clearly showing grooves cut by iron wagon wheels.

REFRESHMENTS:
The White Horse Inn, Holtye.

Walk 21 WINCHELSEA AND THE ROYAL MILITARY CANAL   5m (8km)

Maps: OS Sheets Landranger 189; Pathfinder 1291.

A walk around a once busy, now sleepy, town, and past a defensive system that was never tested.

Start: At 906176, St Thomas' Church, Winchelsea.

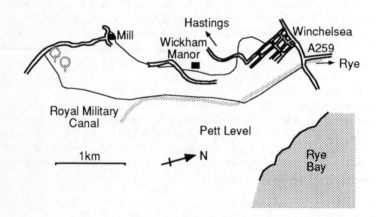

Go out of the north-west corner of the churchyard, near the New Inn, and turn south, passing a bus shelter and walking to a cross-roads. Turn right. Go straight ahead at the next junction and then cross a sports field. Go over a stile, and after a further 25 yards, turn half-left, downhill. Go through two gates and then turn left to return to the main road. Cross with care, and turn right along a path. At the next path junction go left, then cross towards a ruin. Just before reaching this, go over a stile, and descend, going over several more stiles to reach a gate and stile. Just to the left here is the edge of the old town's defensive ditch and the site of New Gate. Go over the stile and walk uphill, heading south-westwards, to Wickham Manor, passing it on your right. Now maintain direction for a further 400 yards, going over several stiles to reach Wickham Rock Lane. Cross, go through the gate opposite and walk towards a line of trees. Pass the trees on your right and then aim towards the mill on the little hill ahead to rejoin the lane. Keep left along the lane for about 80 yards, then go right through a gate. Climb up past the mill, to the left, then go downhill to reach a stile. Go over on to a road. Go left along the road to reach a T- junction. The mill is on your left here, with Elms Farm on your right. Turn right at the T-junction and follow Pett Lane, for about $^3/_4$ mile ($1^1/_4$kms). Shortly after passing a path on the right leading to Knockbridge, and after passing a small wood to the left, go left along the southern edge of the wood, following a stream eastwards across Pett Marshes. The path uses several footbridges as it crosses the marshes, and then swings north-east to reach Wickham Cliff. Here too, the route is joined, from the south, by the **Royal Military Canal**. Walk along the canal's left bank for $^1/_2$ mile ($^3/_4$kms), then cross to the right bank via a concrete bridge. Now follow the right bank to reach a road. Turn left towards **Winchelsea** and keep ahead, passing The Bridge public house. Maintain direction for a further short distance, then go left up steps. At the top, go on, near Strand Gate, then go left reach to the church, on the right.

POINTS OF INTEREST:
Royal Military Canal – The canal was, most oddly, dug (30 feet wide!) to repel a possible Napoleonic invasion in the early 1800's. It seems hardly likely to have deterred seasoned troops who had crossed such obstacles as the Danube, the Rhine and, by the time they landed here, the English Channel. The canal cost £200,000 – quite a sum in those days.

Winchelsea – This was once a busy seaport (the old sea cliffs are still clearly visible on this walk, which passes below them) but the sea destroyed it in 1287. The port was rebuilt, but was often attacked and plundered by the French. After the harbour silted up the population, once 6000, fell: it is now just a few hundred. St Thomas' Church is well worth exploring. The 1930 stained glass tells the town's story graphically. Note too 'Wesley's Tree', under which the famous Methodist preacher gave his last sermon.

REFRESHMENTS:
The New Inn, Winchelsea.
The Bridge, Winchelsea.

Walk 22   RUSHLAKE GREEN   5m (8km)

Maps: OS Sheets Landranger 199; Pathfinder 1290.

High Weald country, mostly field paths, but sometimes muddy!

Start: At 627184, the Horse and Groom Inn, Rushlake Green.

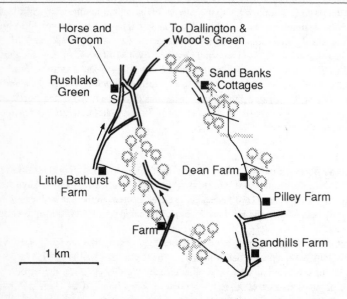

From the inn walk to the road signposted 'Wood's Corner' and head north-eastwards along it for 400 yards. Now fork right, going over a stile, then bearing half-left to reach a second stile. Go over and keep ahead, passing a pond, to the left, towards woodland. Keeping the trees on your left, bear right and walk beside some cottages, to the left. Walk down to another stretch of woodland. Now keep on the drive ahead but soon, in front of a gate, turn right (the ruins of a **Priory** are just to the left here). Descend along a field edge and then take a track into more trees. Cross a stream and go left, uphill a little. Maintain direction (south-eastwards) to reach a concrete lane at the buildings of Dean Farm. Go to the right of the farm, then keep right to go alongside several fields. At the bottom, go left, alongside both a stream and some trees until it is possible to turn right over the water. Walk up across three small fields, with stiles between them, keeping to the right of a house (Pilley Farm), and taking a drive down to a lane. Turn right to a junction. Turn left, passing Sandhills Farm, to reach a point where the lane from Dallington joins from the left. Here, look for a post box to the left, and take the drive opposite. After about 100 yards, go right between buildings and through two gates. Go over a stile and ascend to a trig point. Cross a stile in the nearby field corner and, keeping left of a pond, go through a gate. Cross a field beyond and go over a stile into woods.

Follow the curving woodland path generally north-westwards, keeping right of an enclosure. Next, bear right and then left to reach a pond, on the left. Now cross the wooden railings, and go left on a wide path. Go over more railings and ascend to reach Iwood Place at a lane. Cross the lane and almost immediately go left over a stile (maintaining the same direction as before). After 25 yards go half-right to descend a field to a stile in the bottom right corner, with trees to the left. Go over the stile and follow waymarks on further stiles. Go over a drive, then go to the left of a house and along the right side of a field. When you see a stile on the right leading down to a road, do not go over: instead turn left to descend into another wood. Now, keep walking westwards. Cross a footbridge and then turn half-right, with the wood to the right. Emerging into more open land, go across the field ahead to reach a stile. Go over and bear half-left across two more fields to reach a drive. Follow this for a few yards to reach a road. Turn right along the road, ignoring the back lane forking right, to arrive back in **Rushlake Green**.

POINTS OF INTEREST:

Rushlake Green – This is an attractive village with a raised triangular green bordered by brick cottages, houses and a few shops. Nearby is the Priory Hotel and what's left of an Augustinian Priory, founded in 1413 but dissolved by Henry VIII. Morbid or curious customers can open wooden shutters to see what are said to be the skulls of two monks.

REFRESHMENTS:

The Horse and Groom, Rushlake Green.
There is also a Tearoom in the village.

Walk 23   OLD HASTINGS AND FAIRLIGHT GLEN   5m (8km)

Maps: OS Sheets Landranger 199; Pathfinder 1291.

The old fishing port and a classic coastal walk.

Start: At 825094, on Hastings seafront.

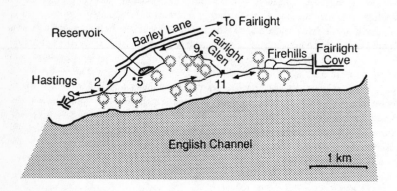

After pausing to explore the many interesting features in the neighbourhood, walk past the Dolphin Inn and then ascend the Tamarisk Steps to reach Lindsell Cottages. Go up the steps to the right and continue to the summit of the funicular railway. Now follow the bollard-signed coastal path with, at first, sports fields to the left, continuing for about 2 miles to reach 'Lover's Seat' near bollard 11.

An extra, but very scenic mile, plus a mile to return, can be added here by walking forward, through the shrubby clifftops of 'Firehills', until the built up part of Fairlight is reached. Now about turn and walk back to bollard 11.

From bollard 11, we turn inland along the wooded valley to reach bollard 9, following signs to Upper Fairlight Glen and Barley Lane. To continue, go along a track between fences to reach the metalled Barley Lane. Turn left (south-westward) for 600 yards and, opposite a footpath signed 'Ore', to the right, go left on an unsigned

O'Shea, P.L. and B.M.   *100 Walks in East Sussex*   ISBN 1 85223 807 0

Erratum
The numbering on the county map (page 7) is incorrect; the correct version is reproduced here.

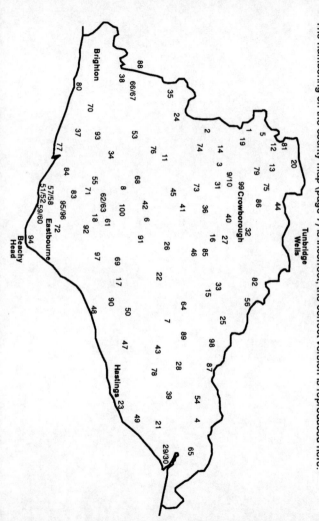

path for about 50 yards, then cross the stile ahead, ignoring the path's left fork into a garden. Walk into the wood ahead. After about 200 yards of woodland walking, descend, forking right to pass Ecclesbourne Reservoir, on the right.

About 200 yards past the reservoir, at bollard 5, follow the sign for 'Barley Lane', to the right. Cross a stream, then ascend to a stile just before reaching the lane again. Now go left and walk across open country, with the valley on your left, until the original coast path is rejoined near bollard 2. Now return to old **Hastings** with its net houses, but a diminishing number of fishing boats.

POINTS OF INTEREST:

Hastings – Do not miss the tall black wooden 'net shops' where local fishermen hang their nets to dry. Up the Tamarisk Steps is Tackleway where a plaque at No. 27 informs you that the poet and novelist George McDonald resided here. Main Street, Old Humphrey Avenue and All Saints Church are all fascinating. Dante G. Rossetti lodged and married in Hastings (see the Cutter Hotel for more details). There is also The Castle housing an audio visual show – 'The 1066 Story', – St Stephen's Caves (smugglers' caves and a geological curiosity) and The Embroidery (depicting great moments in the last nine-hundred years). The local Town Guide has more details for the walker or student of architecture and literature.

REFRESHMENTS:

There is a fine variety of hostelries and cafés – and a selection of candy floss, cockles and whelks – in Hastings.

Maps: OS Sheets Landranger 198; Pathfinder 1268.
Mostly open heathland near the border with West Sussex.
Start: At 382211, on the A272 west of North Chailey.

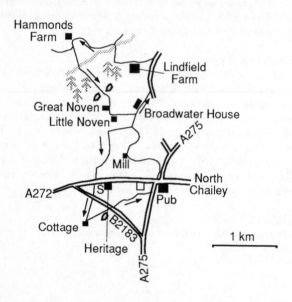

With your back to the **Chailey Heritage** on the A272, walk forward, westwards, with care, and after passing the School sign turn left along a narrow path through a scrubby area to reach the B2183. Almost opposite is a 'private footpath': take this to reach a cottage. Turn left along its edge, going past a pond to reach the B2183 once again. Cross and maintain the same easterly direction across the common, with a playing field to the left, to reach the village of North Chailey. Turn left to reach a junction with the A272. Cross into the village car park to find a path parallel to the A275. Walk north on this path, but, after 100 yards, turn left along a tarmac road, then almost at once go half-right and head for a white windmill.

Turn right 80 yards before the mill and walk across the common to reach a trig point. Now head north for 50 yards, then go right along a clear track for 150 yards before turning left and descending towards a stream. When 10 yards short of the stream, turn right and go across two bridges. Now look out for a cottage, to the left, bear left there and then turn right on to a drive. When the drive reaches a tarmac drive, go right and then left on to a grassy path and follow 'reserve' posts, passing to the right of Broadwater House. Continue north-eastwards, going under electricity cables to reach a road. Turn left for 300 yards to reach a sandy path, on the left, to Lindfield Farm. Pass the farm on your left, then follow waymarks over several stiles as you head westward to reach the corner of a wood. Here go right over a stile and walk alongside a field to reach a stream.

Cross the stream and turn left along the Sussex Border Path to reach Hammonds Farm. Just short of the buildings, go left through a wide gateway, leaving the Border Path and heading south. Cross the stream again, then go uphill to pass another wood, on your right. Now go downhill and across an area of raised path between two ponds. About 100 yards further on, go right over a stile, then turn right, under the cables, to reach Great Noven Farm. Go through the buildings and turn left along the farm's access drive. This leads to the drive on the approach to Broadwater House passed earlier in the walk. Turn right, passing Little Noven and continuing to reach the Common once more. Soon, you leave the outward route to walk west along the Common's northern edge. After about 500 yards turn southwards towards the start of the walk, keeping 400 yards to the west of the windmill away to the left. Bear slightly right to return to the start.

POINTS OF INTEREST:

North Chailey and Chailey Heritage – This area is considered to be the very centre of Sussex (East and West), the walk straying into West Sussex. The Common has a wide variety of heathland plants – heather, gorse and orchids. The stonechat might be seen in the area too. The Heritage School is world famous as a training centre for spina bifida and cerebral palsy sufferers and other severely crippled children.

REFRESHMENTS:

The King's Head Inn, North Chailey. The Inn is at the crossroads of the A272 and the A275.

Walk 25   ETCHINGHAM AND SWIFTSDEN   5m (8km)

Maps: OS Sheets Landranger 199; Pathfinder 1270.

A quiet walk through woods and fields north-east of Etchingham.

Start: At 715263, Etchingham Station car park.

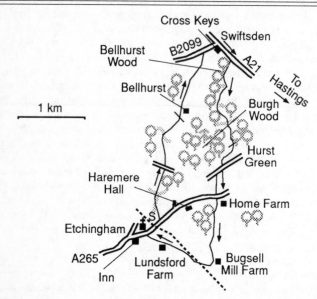

From the station car park, **Etchingham**, turn left and go over the level crossing. Go over two bridges, then turn left and go down steps to reach a stream. Keep the stream on your left until a bridge enables you to cross it. Continue northwards, re-crossing the stream after about 350 yards and then walking ahead to reach a gate in a field corner. Go through to a lane and cross straight over to reach a gate. Go through and cross two fields. The track now becomes indistinct, but look out for the stream again, to the right, and follow it into the next field. Cross a little bridge and follow a path uphill. Cross another track and continue ahead, the path becoming firmer as it reaches Bellhurst. Continue along the track to reach the B2099. Turn right, and right again on reaching the B2099's junction with the busy A21 at the Cross Keys Inn.

Walk along the A21, with great care, to reach a caravan site. There, turn right through an iron gate into a paddock. Cross this, and a field, with Bellhurst Wood on your right. Maintain a south-westward direction, but then curve left around a pond and barn, before dropping down and bearing left to enter a wood. Cross a stream within the wood and, on the far side, climb steeply up through the trees (of Burgh Wood). Soon, bear left, then gently right, still climbing, to go through an open area of coppiced trees, continuing to reach the outskirts of Hurst Green. Turn right behind the long back gardens and, in due course, a twitten appears between two houses. Use this to reach a road. (Refreshments are available in Hurst Green: turn left along the road. The detour will add a mile to the walk length.)

Turn right along the road for about 200 yards, then cross and go left, southerly, between gardens, walk along the right side of a field, with a wood to the right, and continue to reach the very busy A265 again. Turn left, with care, then cross, with even more care, and turn right on to the access drive to Home Farm. Follow this for almost a mile, going past Grove Wood, to the right, and eventually reaching a junction of paths by Bugsell Mill Farm. Go through the gate on the right, and walk downhill across a field to reach a stream and a railway crossing. Turn right, following the line, then veer left, and away from the railway, to go over a concrete bridge. Walk towards, and go to the right of Lundsford Farm. Cross the farm drive by way of a stile and follow the sign to Etchingham to arrive back at the A265 close to the welcoming Arms! Turn right to reach the railway station and start point.

POINTS OF INTEREST:

Etchingham – The church of the Assumption and St Nicholas, close to the railway station, is much as it was when first completed in 1363, though it was once moated. It contains a fine collection of carvings and brasses.

Nearby is Haremere Hall where shire-horses can be admired (Tel: 058 081501).

REFRESHMENTS:

The Cross Keys, Swiftsden.
The Etchingham Arms, Etchingham.

Walk 26   CADE STREET AND WARBLETON   5¹/₄m (8¹/₂km)

Maps: OS Sheets Landranger 199; Pathfinders 1290, 1270 and 1269.

Woods and farmland in the Sussex Weald with artistic and historical associations, two churches, a chapel and three pubs.
Start: At 614206, Cade Street Chapel on the B2096.

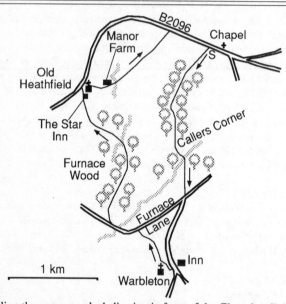

After reading the monument's dedication in front of the **Chapel** walk back towards the village (westward) a hundred yards or so to reach a gate on the left which leads to a footpath. At the bottom of the field crossed by the path, go through a second gate into another field. Look for, and go through, a gate on the right and bear right towards some trees. Go through a fourth gate into woods, and, very soon, turn left. Go forward 50 yards, and then fork left. The new path heads south through the woods, going through a wooden gate with a house on the right. Go around and behind the house and descend to reach a stream at Caller's Corner. Go past the bridge with the iron gate on the right, and down the path to cross the next bridge. Now ascend to reach the junction of two roads. Go straight over, on the top road, and follow it to **Warbleton**.

Go through the churchyard and leave by the top right north-east corner. Go diagonally across a large field with a view to a fine valley and Heathfield Church (**Turner**). On the far side of the field go through a hedge gap on to Furnace Lane. Turn left and follow the lane as it bends left and right a little, and crosses a stream. About 200 yards past the stream turn right into a field with a farmhouse in the top left-hand corner. The path passes in front of the buildings and then goes along the left side to reach a gate and path, on the left. Follow the path up to a gate. Go through and keep close to Furnace Wood, to the left, continuing along an avenue to reach a gate in the next field. After about 40 yards, go over a stile on the right, and walk across to reach a gate at the top of the field. There is a house on the right, behind a fence: go along this fence to reach a gate. Go through on to a path that goes around the house. Bear left to reach the road in Old Heathfield, a village with a fine church and inn. Take the footpath behind the church, going north-east and over a footbridge. Go past Manor Farm and uphill along the right edge of five fields on a clear track that leads to the B2096. Turn right along the road to rejoin the Chapel.

POINTS OF INTEREST:

Cade Street Chapel – During the reign of Mary Tudor – a Catholic – ten Protestants were burned at the stake in Lewes. Four were locals, from Warbleton and Cade Street. Jack Cade has his memorial in the village back along the B2096. He led a revolt in 1450 but was pursued – probably to this area – and slain.

Warbleton – A visit to the village church, St Mary's, is a must – so many fascinating relics to see.

Turner – The renowned landscape painter (1775-1851) appreciated and painted the view from Warbleton churchyard across the valley to Heathfield. The prospect has hardly changed since his day. To check that, you can view the painting in London's Tate Gallery.

REFRESHMENTS:

The War-bill-in-tun, Warbleton.
The Star Inn, Old Heathfield.
The Jack Cade, Cade Street.

Walk 27 **MAYFIELD** $5\frac{1}{4}$m ($8\frac{1}{2}$km)

Maps: OS Sheets Landranger 199; Pathfinder 1269.

A look at Mayfield and the wood and farmland to the north. Uphill and down dale.

Start: At 587269, Mayfield village car park.

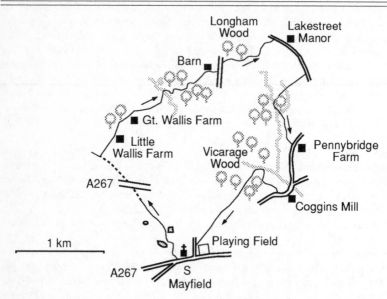

This walk combines readily with Walk 16 to make a longer figure-of-eight centred on **Mayfield**.

Leave the car park by walking northwards, back into the High Street, and there turn left, going along the A267 for about 100 yards. Turn right into North Street and go past the churchyard. Maintain direction passing the edge of three fields and going between ponds to reach a disused railway line which goes under the main road. Continue for a further 200 yards to reach a drive leading half-right to Little, and then Great, Wallis Farm. This is a good section of walking, going into a valley and then reaching a high fence built to keep out deer. Cross a little stream and go over a stile in the fence 120 yards further on. Go forward to reach a gap in the fence. Now ascend through woodland to reach a stile. Go over and walk up and along the field edge. At

58

the left corner, go through another gap, then half-right and over a stile. Keep going uphill, with trees to the right, making for a barn. Pass the barn on your left and continue to reach a road.

Turn left, walking past a college entrance and, after another 150 yards, cross a stile on the right and descend half-right between areas of woodland. Go through the gate into the woodland ahead and pick up a track descending between banks to reach a squeeze stile leading to the corner of a field. Go straight ahead, with more woodland to the left, and after another 100 yards go through a gate and along a garden path (yes, it is a public path!) to reach a lane. Turn right along the lane to a point opposite the entrance to Harewood House. Now go over a stile on the right. Go downhill and leap(!) a small stream at the bottom. Go up the left edge of the next field and at the field corner, go over a stile into a wood. Climb between banks continue to reach a lane by Pennybridge Farm.

Turn right along the lane to reach Coggins Mill. At a T-junction go right, and right again after a further 400 yards into the drive by the pumping station. When the drive divides, go right, along the fence, and through woodland to reach a little bridge. Do not cross: instead, bear left and ascend a sunken track through the woods to emerge into farmland again. Keep along the left edge of three fields, heading south-westerly, cross over a drive and maintain direction along a hedge of holly. As the path bears right, keep straight ahead, going up a bank into the village playing field. Another 200 yards brings you back to the school, the A267 and the start of the walk.

POINTS OF INTEREST:

Mayfield – In addition to enjoying the delightful buildings and High Street – Middle House is an oak-beamed Tudor Inn, 1575 – note the village sign portraying a young maid (Maid's Field). The story goes that St Dunstan, a blacksmith, was at his forge when the Devil, disguised as a beautiful maiden, attempted to seduce him but noticing 'she' had cloven hoofs grabbed 'her' nose with his hot tongs causing 'her' to leap into Tunbridge Wells, cooling her poor nose in the springs. Hence the sulphurous and healing waters! The tongs are shown to visitors at the Catholic Convent of the Holy Child nearby, together with St Dunstan's anvil.

REFRESHMENTS:
None en route, but Mayfield is well-endowed.

Walk 28   SEDLESCOMBE AND CRIPP'S CORNER   5$\frac{1}{2}$m (9km)

Maps: OS Sheets Landranger 199; Pathfinder 1290 and 1270.

Woodland tracks and Wealden footpaths.

Start: At 777188, Sedlescombe Church, $\frac{3}{4}$ mile north of the village.

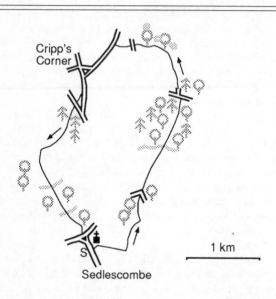

Just a little south of the church of **St John the Baptist, Sedlescombe** take the path between 'Castleman's Oast' and 'Coach House' to reach a stile. Cross and descend to a footbridge. Cross and go up to reach another stile under power lines. Do not cross: instead, go left, with a hedge on your right, to go over the next stile. Continue to a gate, go through and turn right, then left on a wide track to reach a house, 'Woodstock'. Here go half-left on a path (this is a waymark on a pole) to reach a road. Go straight over to a hydrant sign and continue northwards down a track to reach a waymarked gate and stile. Cross and descend to another stile. Cross and head first for a waymarked pole in the middle of a field then for the woods ahead, reaching another waymark.

Go through a gate into the wood and ascend, passing an old building as the country opens out, and eventually reaching a gate on to a road. Go left, then cross the road into the lane opposite, following it down for about 200 yards. As the lane bends right, go left on a footpath into a field. Keeping the hedge on your left, go to the top of the field and through an iron gate. Go straight on, with a fence on your right. The path becomes fenced on both sides and leads to a large iron gate: go through, skirt a pond and go through a seven-barred gate into a field. Go directly across, passing under two sets of power lines to reach a gate in the far hedge. Go through, turn left and through another gate. Maintain direction and go over a stile on to a tarmac path. Turn right and walk to a road. Cross and continue straight ahead, with a hedge on the right, to reach a gate between old wartime pillboxes.

Continue alongside a reservoir and waterworks to reach the B2165. Turn left to **Cripp's Corner** and the White Hart Inn, continuing to reach the busy A229. Turn left, with care, along the main road and, at a large sign, turn right into a fenced path, following it through gates to reach a minor road. Cross and go over the stile opposite. Now walk diagonally left across a field to a gate into woodland. Keep to the track along the wood's eastern edge to reach a stile into a field. Go diagonally right to reach a stile in the far corner. Cross, then go over a stream and another stile, and ascend with hedge on your left to reach the next field corner. Go over a stile, then through a gate into a small paddock. About 25 yards ahead there is a stile by the edge of a small copse, to the right of a gate. Cross and go diagonally left across the field beyond to reach the end of a line of poplar trees. Now enter a small wood and descend to cross a stream. Ascend, bearing right, to reach a stile by a wooden gate. Go over into a field. Go straight across to reach a wooden footbridge over a second stream. Cross this and a stile and go uphill to reach the small wood ahead. With the wood on your left, follow the clear path over the last of the walk's stiles and, soon after, a five-barred gate to reach the main Sedlescombe Road. Cross, turn right and go around a corner to return to the church.

POINTS OF INTEREST:
Sedlescombe Church – Splendid old yews, giant Spanish chestnut trees, some 13th century remains, an octagonal, iron-braced font with an oaken cover raised by a great pulley and a most unusual seating-plan by the door – all are of special note.
Cripp's Corner – In 1432 John Cryps was a substantial landowner in this area.

REFRESHMENTS:
The Coach and Horses, Sedlescombe.
The White Hart, Cripp's Corner.
There are also other possibilities in Sedlescombe.

Walks 29 & 30 RYE HARBOUR AND WINCHELSEA BEACH $5\frac{1}{2}$m (9km) or 8m (13km)

Maps: OS Sheets Landranger 189; Pathfinder 1291.

Along the foreshore and back along flooded gravel pits, with an optional visit to Camber Castle.

Start: At 941191, the car park in Rye Harbour.

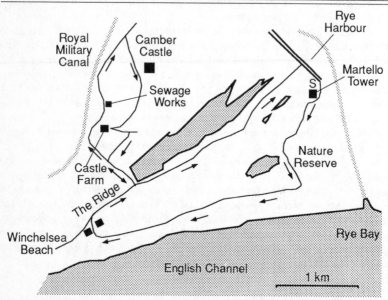

Leaving the **Rye Harbour** car park turn right, seawards, passing a Martello Tower and going into the Caravan Park. Soon, fork left on to a grassy bank, cross a concrete sluice and, after about 400 yards, by a fenced area, go left and into the Nature Reserve. At the first 'lake', turn left and walk down to the beach. At high tide the walk will be shingly or on the flood barrier, but at all events a mile of beach walking stretches westward to **Winchelsea Beach**. Just short of a grassy bank, about 500 yards from the Lifeboat Station, leave the beach going between two small flooded pits and then turning sharp right again. This is 'The Ridge', and there are buildings and gardens to the left. After a further 500 yards, a large flooded pit inland is reached. The longer variant to this walk goes out to **Camber Castle** from here, returning to this same point.

For that longer walk, turn left, away from the sea, with the lake on the right. Walk for about 500 yards to reach a rough road, Morlais Ridge. Cross the stile in the fence ahead and continue to go over another stile and a footbridge. Go through a gate and follow a power line to reach another gate. Here, go right, then left on a short section of path on to a tarmac road. Turn right along the road, but keep left at a fork (do not go to Castle Farm and do not go to the sewage works). The way forward is now to go between the stream and the **Royal Military Canal**, with Rye on the high ground head. About $\frac{1}{2}$ mile ($\frac{3}{4}$kms) after passing the sewage works, turn off the path sharply right and go over a culvert towards **Camber Castle**. Pass to the right of the Castle – turn off left here if you wish to visit – following the path as it curves round to the right towards the rear of Castle Farm. About 100 yards short of the farm go very sharply left – almost back on yourself – on to a track, with a fence to the right. After a further 200 yards go over a stile on the right, and follow the edge of the field beyond. You are now heading seawards again: go through a gate, and the path back at The Ridge, rejoining the shorter walk, with the lake now on the left.

Turn left towards Rye Harbour and walk with the Channel off to the right, and the lakes with their islands to the left, to reach a road. Turn right along the road to return to the car park.

POINTS OF INTEREST:

Rye Harbour – The harbour is a fascinating and colourful place for those who love messing about with boats. The Martello Tower is one of many which were built to repel a possible Napoleonic invasion. The name derives from Cape Mortella in Corsica where the original tower of this design was built. During the walk through the Nature Reserve, look out for the numerous seabirds.

Winchelsea Beach – Winchelsea was an important coastal town in the 12th century but a storm, raids from the French and the silting up of the harbour has now left the town marooned inland, an attractive relic of former splendours.

Royal Military Canal – The canal, which runs from Hythe to the Isle of Oxney, was dug at the time of possible Napoleonic invasion, both as a defensive 'moat' and to transport soldiers and supplies.

Camber Castle – The castle was built by Henry VIII as a defence from invasion following his break with the Roman Catholic church. It is now a ruin having been dismantled in 1642. Once on a peninsula jutting out into the Channel, it is now a mile inland.

REFRESHMENTS:
None en route but plenty available in Rye.

Walk 31 POUNDGATE AND HIGH HURSTWOOD $5^{1}/_{2}$m (9km)

Maps: OS Sheets Landranger 198; Pathfinder 1269.
Edge of Ashdown Forest, undulating but easy-going.
Start: At 482285, Poundgate car park.

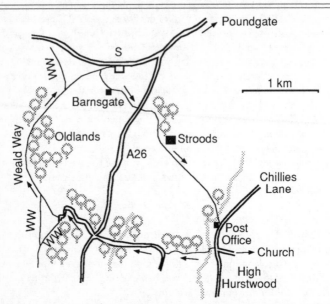

Cross the bar and, at the back of the car park, go over a ditch to reach a path running southwards. As this bends left, go right through the bracken. Keep right to reach the edge of a vineyard, then go left, through a gate, to pass in front of the restaurant of **Barnsgate Manor**. Now ascend, leftwards, to reach a car park and an access drive leading to the main road (the A26). Cross over carefully and go up the drive opposite. This leads to 'Stroods', which is passed to the right (Path 23), beside two field gates. Cross the stile to the left of the left-hand gate and continue south-eastwards – the village of High Hurstwood can be seen ahead – across fields by way of stiles. Now go downhill to reach an enclosed path, and follow it over a footbridge then up, fairly steeply, to reach Chillies Lane.

 Turn right, down the lane to reach a turn, to the left, which leads to the church in High Hurstwood. Do not go left here: instead, turn right over a stile, and go through the wood. Go over a footbridge and a stile into a field. Ascend towards a lone tree, then go over another stile and along the next field hedge to reach a stile on to a lane. Follow the lane to reach the busy A26 again. Cross, with care, and take the lane opposite. Follow the lane to reach the iron gates of Oldlands Hall. Face the gates and turn left along a track and, at the garages, look out for a **WW** (Wealdway) sign which suggests going left. Do not follow the sign: instead, keep ahead along the rough track until you reach a cottage on the right. Opposite this, take a wide path off to the left. The path curves right and runs parallel to the rough track and soon the Wealdway joins from the left, offering reassuring signs for the next $^3/_4$ mile ($1^1/_4$km) as you pass silver birch trees, cross a private drive, and pass cottages, to the right and over a footbridge. Climb up through woodland and go straight over the track by a cottage, going behind it and up along a narrow path to cross the drive again. Go along a narrow path to join the drive yet again. The Wealdway now goes left, but your route curves right (the vineyards are now to the right) to return through bracken, to reach the starting car park.

POINTS OF INTEREST:
Barnsgate Manor – This 56 acre farm, with wonderful views across the Weald to the South Downs, has 12 acres of vines, and offers wine-tasting and sales. There are also llamas and donkeys, a gift shop, tearooms and a restaurant. Guided tours can be arranged, (Tel: 0825 713366) for information.

REFRESHMENTS:
The restaurant and tearooms at Barnsgate Manor.
The Crow and Gate Inn, Poundgate (about 1 mile east of the start).

Walk 32   TOWN ROW AND THE HIGH WEALD   5¹/₂m (9km)

Maps: OS Sheets Landranger 188; Pathfinder 1248.

Hilly heathland and woods west of Wadhurst.

Start: At 567302, carefully in Town Row, ¹/₂ mile north of Rotherfield.

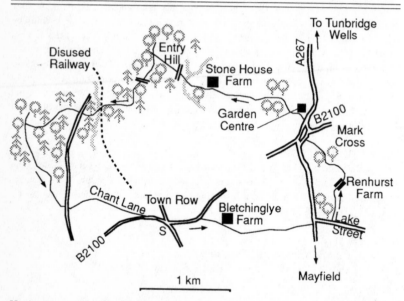

Having located the 'Harvest Moon' pub on the B2100, in Town Row, walk 400 yards eastward and then fork right into Bletchinglye Lane. Follow the lane, ignoring a left turn towards an oast conversion, and descending between banks to reach a stream. Cross, and then leave the lane by going right and crossing a field near Bletchinglye Farm to reach a stile. Go over and maintain direction over several stiles and fields to reach a house and a gate on to the A267.

Turn left, cross, with care, and turn right into Lake Street, with a wood to the left. After 200 yards, as the wood ends, go through a gate on the left, and now head north, going downhill and then rising up to Renhurst Farm. Go between the buildings and, after passing an old oasthouse, go through a gate ahead. Turn left and walk round two sides of the field beyond to reach another gate. Go through and walk along the hedge on the right to reach the village of Mark Cross. Go past the village inn and then cross over the A267, again with care. Now keep the Garden Centre on your right and enter the field ahead. The route is now westward, using stiles and yellow waymarks, to go through a wood. Emerging, from the wood, go over a stile, and then walk beside a bank on the right, going across fields with stiles (four of them) and gates (two) to reach more woodland. During this section of the walk you will pass Stone House Farm, to the right.

Go 50 yards into the wood, then left, downhill, to reach a little bridge. Cross and climb up to a lane running left and right. Cross straight over and keep ascending for another 400 yards, passing a cottage and stables, to reach a meeting point of four tracks. Go left, still uphill, and on reaching the summit fork right and continue to reach a lane. Go right, and shortly left on a path that descends through trees and heathland. Go under an old railway line and over a stream, continuing to reach a road. Cross and climb up through conifers and heathland, crossing a wide firebreak with a fire warning notice. Now keep to the path with a fence to the left and trees to its right until another fire warning notice is reached. Here turn right, and shortly left, to enter woodland. Keep southerly and descend, going over a stile and across a field. In the right-hand corner of the field you will reach a drive: follow this to a road. Turn right, but soon go left on to a sunken track (Chant Lane), following it to reach the B2100. Turn left and follow the road back to Town Row.

REFRESHMENTS:
The Harvest Moon, Town Row.
The Mark Cross Inn, Mark Cross.

Walk 33   **STONEGATE STATION**   5¹/₂m (9km)

Maps: OS Sheets Landranger 199; Pathfinder 1270.

A fine walk in the Sussex High Weald and across the Rother Valley.

Start: At 659272, Stonegate Station.

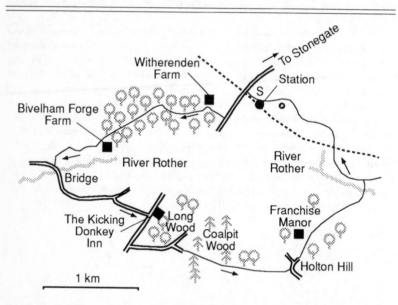

From the railway station return to the road and turn left. Cross the railway line and, after about 400 yards, turn right to Witherenden Farm. Go left, through the buildings, then ahead along a track. Go through a gate and descend to cross a brook over a concrete bridge. Take the track beyond, going across a field and through a gate to enter Newbridge Wood. Keep to the narrow path in the wood, heading south-westwards for almost a mile (about 1¹/₄kms). Leave the wood and go past Bivelham Forge Farm, taking its access drive down to a lane. Turn left and follow this usually quiet lane across the River Rother. Stay on the lane as it ascends to reach a junction. Turn right and, soon after, left, going up and then gently down to reach the Kicking Donkey Inn at another junction.

Turn right along a lane for 400 yards, then go left along Spring Lane. After another 400 yards the lane forks: go right here, opposite a house, walking downhill along the right edge of a field. At the bottom of the hill, go ahead into woodland. Cross a track to follow a narrow path which soon bears left, becomes wider and crosses a culvert. About 20 yards further on, bear right and go uphill, through woodland, to reach a stile. Go over and ascend further, passing a barn and keeping ahead to reach a gap in a hedge. Go through and bear slightly left, following the hedge on the left. Turn left through a gate beside a power-pole, and after about 50 yards, turn right along a tarmac drive. When the drive turns left, keep straight ahead, going through a gate and then heading downhill with a hedge on your right.

Continue by going through a gate into a little wood and then going uphill to reach the top left-hand corner of a field: Go through a gate on to a track and turn left turn to reach a road at Holton Hill. Turn left, forking right soon after to go along an avenue. Ignore crossing tracks, but keep straight on when a drive goes left towards Franchise Manor. Maintain direction (north-easterly) downhill, walking with railings to the left, then go through a kissing-gate and walk with a hedge to the right to descend to a field corner. Turn left and cross the River Rother on Wreckery Bridge. Continue to reach a T-junction of bridlepaths. Turn left, and keep left along two field edges to reach an enclosed path. Follow the path uphill to reach a railway line. Cross the line and turn left, then veer right to cross a stream. Now follow a path uphill to reach an enclosed track leading to Hammerden Farm. Walk to the left of a pond and continue to the railway station where the walk began.

REFRESHMENTS:
The Kicking Donkey Inn, on the route.
Refreshments are also available at Stonegate Station.

Walk 34 GLYNDE, CABURN AND BIBLE BOTTOM 5½m (9km)

Maps: OS Sheets Landranger 198; Pathfinder 1308 and 1289.

A hilly walk, an attractive village, an Iron Age fort and stunning views.

Start At 456094, in the village of Glynde.

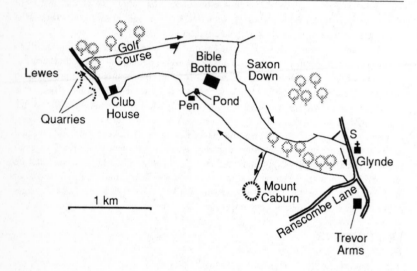

Walk southwards along **Glynde's** village street and turn right into Ranscombe Lane. Go 20 yards past the Post Office, to the left, then go over a stile, on the right. Go uphill and over several stiles to reach a crossing track. Turn left and follow the track to reach **Mount Caburn** hillfort. After exploring and enjoying the views – with the South Downs and Firle Beacon to south and east, the Ouse valley below and Lewes westward, plus the English Channel – return to the track junction and go left to continue along the valley bottom, with the **Bible earthworks** to your right.

Descend to pass between a cattle pen, left, and a dewpond, right. Now go right, then over a stile and on, along the fence on the left, for 200 yards, to reach another stile. Go over and continue along the valley, now heading westward. The path ascends – always keep to the higher track when there is a choice – with a barbed wire fence to

70

the left. Go over stiles and through gates, then across a field to reach the Lewes Golf Course Clubhouse. Turn right along the club's access road – **Lewes** is to your left and below you – and follow it to some trees. Fork right, and then go right again up steps near an obelisk. Continue steeply, up to a ridge and go eastwards along the golf course edge. Beware of flying golf balls, but enjoy the views northwards towards Barcombe and Ringmer.

The track along the course edge is well waymarked with posts. At the fifth green leave the course over a stile and go along the hillside (with Bible Bottom below and to the right) to reach another stile. Go over and walk up to a third stile. Go over and continue along the ridge to reach a crossing track in a little depression. Do not fork left: instead go a little right to a gate and stile. Go over – cross Saxon Down and follow a path downhill, going to the left of a small copse. When the path forks, keep right and walk easily down to Glynde.

POINTS OF INTEREST:

Glynde – This attractive village has thatch, timber and flint cottages and a building with a horseshoe frontage. Was this once the village smith's? The Georgian church is of knapped flint and has box-pews and hessian-covered interior walls. In the churchyard is the grave of John Ellman who first reared the black-faced South Down sheep from which the great flocks of Australia and New Zealand are descended.

Mount Caburn – In the last century BC several hundred people lived here, inside the security of a bank and ditch. An outer defence was added later, perhaps an anti-Roman device. The site, 491 feet above sea level, commands excellent views to warn of strangers. Many archeological finds from the site can be seen in Lewes Museum.

Bible Bottom Earthworks – The earthworks are so-called because they look like an open book.

Lewes – The County town of East Sussex is set on the River Ouse. The town was one of the earliest to be fortified after 1066. The castle and the modern County Hall are clearly visible from Mount Caburn, but a separate visit should be made to see the 15th century buildings, the local history museum and the living history model next door, Southover Grange – once the home of John Evelyn the 17th century diarist – and, of course, Lewes Castle. The Greenwich Meridian runs across the street between the Pewter Pot and the Black Horse inns (See also the Note to Walk 93).

REFRESHMENTS:

The Trevor Arms, Glynde.

Lewes has a full range of possibilities, including the *Pewter Pot* and *Black Horse Inns* which lie in opposite hemispheres as a result of the Greenwich Meridian.

Walk 35 DITCHLING COMMON AND NORTH AMERICA 5½m (9km)

Maps: OS Sheets Landranger 198; Pathfinder 1288.

Easy walking along field paths. Plus two puzzles.

Start: At 339180, Ditchling Common car park on the B2113.

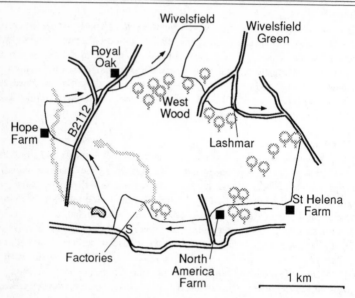

From the car park, walk back along the road, westward, for 250 yards, then head north-west across the common to skirt the little lake, to the left. Go over a stile and, just before a concrete drain, turn right. Go through a gate and then cross open land to reach a scrubby area. Cross a wide track, go through another gate and go on through more scrubland. On the far side of some railings, keep on a narrow track to reach a waymarked post. Turn left and walk to a road (the B2112). Cross the road with care and take the private access road to Ditchling Common Stud, but almost at once cross a stile on the right. Now veer away from the left hedge to cross a field. Keep a pond on your left and cross a little bridge. Go over a stile and continue to reach a drive. Turn right, then almost at once, go left to walk past a house. Go right for 25 yards, then use the drive to go left. Care is now needed: look for a narrow path to the left – it is about 100 yards along the drive – and use it to go through the bracken and low bushes to reach a lane. Cross a lane, then maintain direction to reach the B2112 again. Cross and go along the left edges of two fields. Go over a stile on the left, to return to the road near the Royal Oak, **Wivelsfield**. A short detour to the village should be made if time permits.

Return to the stile opposite the Royal Oak. Go over and turn left. Walk along field edges, going over several stiles to reach a metalled drive. Go left along this and on reaching a lane, turn right. After 50 yards turn right to cross a bridge and stile. Now keep along the left edge of two fields, making for a wood. Follow waymarks into the wood (West Wood), heading eastwards and uphill a little, to reach a lane. Turn right along the lane, but soon turn left along the Lashmar drive, following it to its junction with a road. Turn right along the road. About 100 yards past a right-hand bend, go right, under a rail and across the small field beyond. Go over a plank bridge and then a stile, and follow the hedge to the left, heading due south. At St Helena Farm, turn right and, keeping the buildings on your left, follow the waymarked stiles and go over a footbridge to reach North America Farm, to the left. Go through a garden to reach another stile. Go over and head slightly left to cross a road. Go over the stile opposite and walk along the edge of a field. Go over another stile, then walk left around two sides of a field, before going half-right into the next field. Now cross the Sussex Border Path and go into a small wood. Go right, then left and over a stile to skirt to the north of a factory area. On reaching the more wooded area of the Country Park veer left, and on sighting the pond passed at the start of the walk, go left to reach the road and the car park.

POINTS OF INTEREST:

Wivelsfield – On a tombstone in the belfry chamber of the church is an inscription with two lines upside down! Why? A splendid theory is put forward by Swinfen and Arscott in their excellent book *Hidden Sussex*. The Royal Oak Inn is subtitled Jacob's Post – another conundrum, but one that is more easily explained. The post is part of a gibbet in the Inn's garden. The ghoulish, but amusing, story of the gibbet is well-known 'locally'.

REFRESHMENTS:

The Royal Oak Inn (Jacob's Post), Wivelsfield Green (plus a remedy for toothache!)
The Cock Inn, Wivelsfield Green.

Walk 36   **HADLOW DOWN**   5¹/₂m (9km)

Maps: OS Sheets Landranger 199; Pathfinder 1269.

A quiet valley of the Upper Uck and woodland climb.

Start: At 540241, a lay-by on the A272, ¹/₂ mile east of Hadlow
Down.

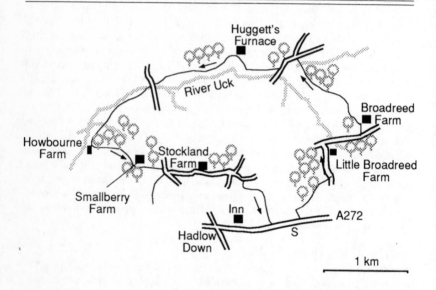

This quiet and peaceful walk begins by crossing the main road. Now, on the left,
shortly after passing Tinker's Lane, to the right, take the track by the entrance to
Little Hadlow. When it veers sharply to the left, about 200 yards further on, go straight
on between banks heading north-eastwards to reach a lane. Turn left and follow the
lane to a T-junction. Turn right for 400 yards, then go left on the access drive to
Broadreed Farm. Bear left at the farm, going between the oasts, left, and the farmhouse,
right. Now drop down between banks and a pond, to the right, to reach a culverted
stream. Cross the culvert and turn left through a gate. Ascend over stiles, going
alongside two fields with woodland to the right and about 10 yards into the third field
turn right through a gate into a wood. You soon emerge from this, going over a stile to
the left: cross straight over the field beyond, walking parallel to a wandering fence on

the right. Descend steeply, then climb up again, going through a plantation to reach a junction of lanes. Turn left, but after 200 yards take the right fork along a clear track to **Huggett's Furnace**. At a farm, go between the buildings and when the track goes right across a cattle grid, go left over a stile and walk ahead to cross another stile in the left field corner.

Continue westwards, with the brown iron-stained waters of the infant River Uck to the left, going through fields to reach a lane running north-south. Go left, cross the Uck and at once go right through a gate. Walk directly ahead across the field beyond to a hedge-gap. Go through and keep a hedge to the right. Pass under electricity wires, go through a second hedge-gap in the corner of the field and maintain direction to reach a gate and a single tree ahead. Keep right in the next field, then go left on a short stretch of path, going uphill and passing to the right of a converted barn. Curve left across the next field to meet the access drive for the barn. After about 10 yards, go through a blue gate, to the left, then go right, walking round two sides of a field and passing a bungalow and pond, right. Maintain direction and, in the far field corner, go through a gap. Ascend with woodland right, to reach Smallberry Hill Farm. Pass to the right of the farm, following the access drive to reach a lane near a crossroads, left. Follow the signpost for 'Rotherfield' to reach a junction of lanes. Ignore the right and left turns (the latter leading to Pig's Foot Farm!), and go steeply downhill. When the lane curves left, go right, into Gillhope Bank Wood. Keep the white wooden railings and a stream on your right and stay with the clear track which climbs left through the wood. Cross a lane and maintain direction along an enclosed path to emerge on to the busy A272. Turn left, with care, using the right-hand verge to return to the lay-by.

POINTS OF INTEREST:

Huggett's Furnace – The smelting of locally mined iron ore was a feature of the Wealden economy from Roman and Celtic times to the 16th and 17th centuries. There were a large number of furnaces and forges utilising charcoal from the nearby forest. The local streams provided the power to work heavy hammers and to temper the metal. The iron was used for cannons, agricultural and domestic tools, firebacks, horseshoes, gravestones etc.

The discovery of coal in great quantity in the north and the subsequent Industrial Revolution meant the rapid decline of the Sussex iron industry. It is now remembered only in such place names as Ashburnham, Furnace Wood, Pond Bay and Burnthouse Farm.

REFRESHMENTS:

The New Inn, Hadlow Down (an architectural oddity $^1/_2$ mile west of the start).

Walk 37   **TELSCOMBE**   5$\frac{1}{2}$m (9km)

Maps: OS Sheets Landranger 198; Pathfinders 1307 and 1308.
Up and down the Downs, behind Peacehaven, to a quiet hamlet.
Start: At 418060, Rodmell village, on the A275 between Lewes
and Newhaven.

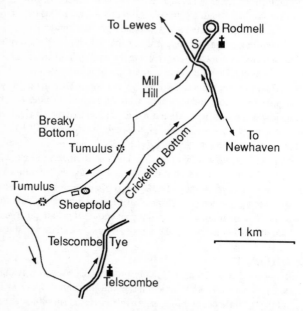

This hilly, usually dry, quiet walk begins in the village of **Rodmell**, which should be
explored.

From the main A275 road take the lane that heads southwards between the little
garage and the White House, ascending to reach a gate on Mill Hill after about $\frac{1}{2}$ mile.
Continue in the same direction for another mile, at first going downhill, then climbing
up again. Go through two gates and walk alongside the fence to the left, to reach a
flint-stone sheepfold, also on the left, and **Breaky Bottom,** the valley to the right. From
the sheepfold continue, with the fence still to the left to reach a gate. Go through and
walk uphill to reach a bridleway T-junction. Here, Highdole Hill is to the right, with
Telscombe Tye to the left.

Go left, heading a little east of south, ignoring all alternatives and enjoying the seaviews. Curve left and head down into **Telscombe**. The walk continues northwards up the road – there are no pubs or shops. About 400 yards out of the hamlet, bear left on to a bridleway and drop into and along Cricketing Bottom. There now follows a simple, 2 mile downland walk, with that timeless feeling of lonely, lark-filled sky and sheep in the flint-walled fields, to regain the busy A275. Turn left along the safety of a grass verge to return to the start.

POINTS OF INTEREST:

Rodmell – A village of thatch, flint and half-timbered homes, with a Norman church. Monk's House was the home of Leonard and Virginia Woolf. In 1941 Virginia, severely depressed, walked down the lane and drowned herself. Leonard died here in 1969. The house is open on Wednesdays and Saturdays in summer. At South Farm there is an ancient mulberry tree, used during the 17th century to establish a local silk industry, silkworms being fed on mulberry leaves.

Breaky Bottom – A vineyard, planted here in 1951, produces an excellent English wine.

Telscombe – The church of St Lawrence has Saxon origins, medieval wall-paintings, a Norman nave and some fine stained-glass windows. It is built on the side of a hill and, as a consequence, part of the churchyard is almost on a level with the church-top. Stud Farm was once a racehorse stable. From it *Shannon Lass* won the 1902 Grand National. The Tye was the gallop area for training the horses. In the Manor House there is accommodation for judges officiating at the Crown Court in Lewes.

REFRESHMENTS:
Nothing en-route but Rodmell has a General Store and the Abergavenny Arms.

Walk 38   **DITCHLING BEACON**   5$^1/_2$m (9km)

Maps: OS Sheets Landranger 198; Pathfinder 1288.

A wonderful walk with splendid views all around.

Start: At 333130, Ditchling Beacon car park.

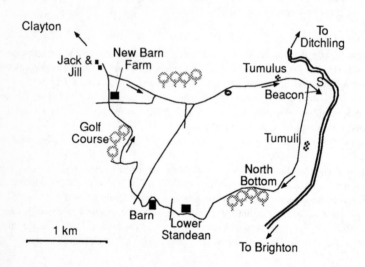

Choose a clear day to enjoy this walk at its best. It is quiet on weekdays, but can be very busy at weekends. Take refreshments!

From the car park at Ditchling **Beacon** walk westwards along the South Downs Way. Below and to the right, is the village of Westmeston, with Ditchling further to the north. Caburn is behind us, as is Firle Beacon, about 11 miles off. Chanctonbury Ring is 12 miles ahead and, on a very clear day, the Hog's Back is visible some 30 miles to the north-west.

On reaching an information board about the nearby Nature Reserve, to the right, turn left and descend gently, bearing right into the valley. Go through a gate at the bottom to enter North Bottom. Now head westwards, then south-westwards, walking past a water trough. Go through two gates and continue, passing to the left of Lower Standean. Turn left and then right, ascending to pass a barn, to the left. Shortly after, turn left, then right again, going through several gates and continue to climb gently. Hereabouts the Sussex Border Path crosses our route because we have indeed strayed into West Sussex. So go north-westwards, passing through another gate and walk with a fence on the right to reach a bridleway. At the next gate turn left and after another 200 yards turn right alongside the Pyecombe Golf Course (to the left). Beware errant golf balls flying out of bounds, followed, perhaps, by angry golfers!

The route continues alongside the course, heading northwards towards two windmills. Just before New Barn Farm, to the right, the walk crosses the South Downs Way and then descends along a bridleway to reach **Jack and Jill**. From here, refreshments are available in **Clayton** – follow the sign in the far corner of the windmill car park: it is about 600 yards downhill, but, of course, uphill on the way back!

After a visit to Jill (Jack is a private house) retrace your steps to an iron gate then walk eastwards to rejoin the South Downs Way. Almost 2 miles (3 kms) of splendid ridge walking now lies ahead, returning you to the Ditchling Beacon car park. Note, en-route, the Keymer Post on the County Border, beautifully lettered and acorned.

POINTS OF INTEREST:

Ditchling Beacon – This is the third highest point on the South Downs Way, and was one of many beacon sites where fires were lit to warn of invaders. The Beacon shows clear traces of an Iron Age hill fort.

Jack and Jill – Jill, the white building, is a post mill once sited at Patcham, north of Brighton and brought over the Downs by oxen. Now restored, the mill is open on Sunday afternoons. Jack is a brick tower mill.

Clayton – If you can spare the time to make the detour to the village, seek out the entrance to the railway tunnel – a fantastic Victorian facade. In the nearby church there are some fine medieval wall-paintings. The royal dress designer Norman Hartnell is buried in the graveyard.

REFRESHMENTS:

The Jack and Jill Inn, Clayton.

There is usually an ice cream van in the starting car park. Otherwise, the suggested detour to Clayton must be followed.

Walk 39   **BREDE**   5$^1/_2$m (9km)

Maps: OS Sheets Landranger 199; Pathfinders 1291 and 1271.

A gently undulating walk with fine valley views.

Start: At 825183, Red Lion Inn, Brede.

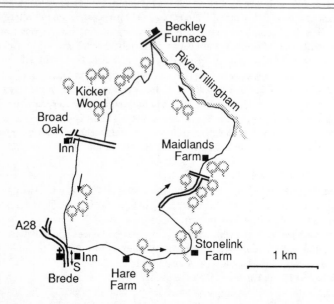

Find time at the start or finish of the walk to visit **St George's Church, Brede** where the journey begins. The Red Lion Inn is conveniently placed on the right.

Walk north for 50 yards, then turn right into a lane, going down it to reach a kissing-gate 50 yards past the last house on the right. Go through and continue generally eastward, going through trees, then over a drive and a stile into a field. Walk down to the gate at the bottom, go through and walk with hedge on your left to reach another gate and stile. Cross the stile and turn left by the farmhouse. Soon you will come to a gate by a cattle grid: go through and walk down the field beyond, with a fence to the left to reach the next stile. Cross, go over a stream and ascend with a fence and hedge to the left. Go through two iron gates to reach an access drive. Cross to the path opposite. Go straight on to reach the field's left corner and, with a hedge to the left, maintain direction to reach a stile. Cross and ascend (with the hedge still to the left) to

80

reach another stile by a signpost. Go over and walk ahead to reach the access track of Stonelink Farm. Turn left. Go past a cottage, to the left and, after about 100 yards, bear left to reach a stile in a hedge. Go over, cross a footbridge and then go uphill with hedge on your left. When this hedge turns left, keep straight on, crossing the field to the opposite hedge. Now keep this on your right and then follow a garden boundary round to a stile in a wire fence. Cross and continue to the garden's corner. There, turn half-right and up to go through a gap in the trees to reach a gate. Go through and turn half-left. Go over a stile, across a drive, over more stiles and walk diagonally across a field to emerge into a lane.

Turn right along the road to reach a T-junction. Turn left, and immediately right into the access lane to Maidlands Farm. Go through the farm buildings and past a cottage into a field. Go down and a little left into the field corner. Go through the wire fence and walk to the left of a little stream, following it until it joins the River Tillingham. There, turn left and follow the riverbank, using small bridges as the track goes from bank to bank, to the road at Beckley Furnace. There, make a sharp left turn and proceed along the right edge of a hop field to an iron gate. Go through and make for the wood ahead. On reaching it, go left and follow edge to reach a gate and stile. Go over and bear right, uphill, to reach a big holly tree and a stile. Go over the stile and follow a fence round to the left to reach another stile. Go over and walk between bungalows to reach a housing estate. Go right, then left (The Martlets) to reach a twitten on to the main road. Turn right and follow the road for 400 yards to reach a kissing-gate on the left by a white painted cottage. Refreshments are available by following the road for a further 150 yards to reach the inn at Broad Oak. Go through the kissing-gate, and follow a path past barns into a field. Now with a hedge to the right, head southwards to reach a stile. Go over to reach another kissing-gate and go through into trees. Next, cross a stile between ponds and maintain direction as you walk close to gardens, to the right. Proceed directly towards Brede's church, ahead, going over more stiles and then along a short path to reach the walk's start.

POINTS OF INTEREST:

St George's Church, Brede – The church was founded in 1140 and within it are found references to the Brede Giant, 7 foot tall and reputed to have eaten a roasted child daily! There are some splendid modern features too, by Sheridan, Monninton and Epstein.

REFRESHMENTS:

The Red Lion Inn, Brede.
The Cross in Hand Inn, Broad Oak.

Walk 40   SOUTH OF ROTHERFIELD   5¹/₂m (9km)

Maps: OS Sheets Landranger 199; Pathfinder 1269.
A Wealden walk with good views.
Start: At 557298, in Rotherfield.

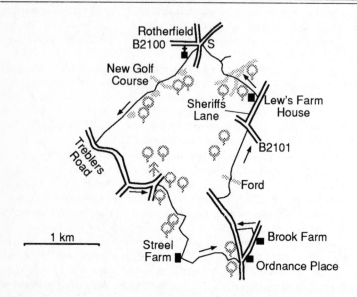

Take the path to the left of the churchyard in **Rotherfield** heading southwards and going through a gate to soon join Court Meadow. Now take the 'twitten' between No. 4 and No. 5, soon passing a pond, to the left, and crossing two fields, where white posts assist the south-west direct route. On reaching the second of two signs, go left and at the approach to a second pond, go right, over the railings. Walk along the left edge of two fields, then go left over a stream. Maintain the south-west direction alongside the stream for about 400 yards to reach, over wire, Treblers Road, a quiet road.

Turn left along the road, following it around a right curve to reach a junction. Turn left and walk to a second junction. Turn sharp right (signpost for Dewland Hill) for about 20 yards, then fork left on to a drive with splendid views south across the Wealden valleys. The drive becomes a narrow path into Castle Wood: walk through the wood and then keep along the left edge of a field.. Walk past a pond, to the left, and go back into trees again. On emerging from the trees we take a farm track to reach the buildings of Streel Farm. Go between these, and then through an iron gate into a field. Go left past a farmhouse and on to the field corner. At the gate, descend to another gate and go across the next field and down to a bridge in a hedge. Cross the bridge and keep to the right of two fields. When about 150 yards up the second field, turn right into a scrubby area. Go over a bridge and walk uphill with a hedge on the right. Walk past posts, to the right, and a little wood to the left and soon after join a track. Follow the track past a garden and a weather-boarded cottage and continue to a lane, Ordnance Place.

Turn left along the lane to reach a fork. Here, take the right-hand lane (Argos Hill) and after passing the last of Brook Farm's buildings, to the right, fork left into a wood. Go through a gate and turn left, going fairly steeply uphill and alongside the wood to reach a fence. Carefully climb over and go half-right across the field, making for a building, to reach a lane opposite Freeman's Farm. Turn right along the lane and, on reaching an electricity sub-station, turn right on to an enclosed track. Follow the track down to a ford, cross the stream and follow a lane (Sheriff's Lane), for almost a mile, crossing the B2101, with care, at Burwood Farm. Now take the access drive to Lew's Farm House, to the left. After 100 yards go left over stiles and then bear right and descend to a bridge. Cross, bear right and go over a stile. Now keep a hedge on your right and walk forward to reach a second stream. Cross and ascend, making for the end of a hedge up and to the right. In the top corner of the field cross a stile and walk with a fence to the left to reach the next corner. Go left over another stile and back into Rotherfield and the start of the walk.

POINTS OF INTEREST:

Rotherfield – St Deny's Church is a very interesting one with 12th century remains, a waggon roof, Jacobean pulpit and an east window with stained-glass by William Morris from designs by Burne-Jones. There are good wall-paintings too. Do not touch the relics of Bertwald: take note of the vengeance threatened on those who do, according to the notes hanging on the wall.

REFRESHMENTS:
The King's Arms, Rotherfield.

Walk 41   **BLACKBOYS**   6m (9½km)

Maps: OS Sheets Landranger 199; Pathfinder 1269.
Easy walking by farm paths and quiet Wealden lanes.
Start: At 522204, the Blackboys Inn, off B2102.

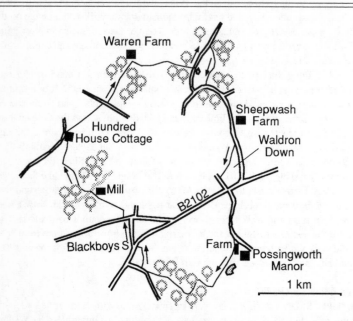

From the inn, in **Blackboys**, go north along School Lane to reach the B2102. Turn left, walk past the bus stop and go right, over a stile, on to a track which runs between allotments to reach a lane. Turn left, and then right at a junction to go down to Tickeridge Mill. Go past the sluice and pond, and through two gates in succession. Now, after 200 yards, at a field corner, turn right and cross two fields with railings, heading straight towards the far corner to reach a lane. Turn right, passing Hundred House Cottage, to the right, and about 50 yards further on turn right again into a copse. Walk along the left side of a field to reach another lane.

Turn right, but soon after, go left towards Warren Farm. After 600 yards, turn right into woodland opposite a garage, taking a path (waymarked thanks to the Sussex Rights of Way Group). Carry straight on, keeping to the left edge of a field, to reach a pond, on the right, and a farm's access road. Take the road to reach a lane and turn left for 400 yards to reach a post box. Opposite the box, turn right along the drive leading to Gill Hope Farm. At the drive's end, wind between the trees, with a garden on the left, then go downhill, passing a cottage to the left, and continuing to reach a lane. Turn left along the lane, passing Sheepwash Farm on the left, and then ascending to Waldron Down. About 250 yards past the access lane to Sheepwash Farm, turn right, over a stile, and walk across the hill, keeping along the left edge of a field, to reach a lane.

Turn left and follow the lane to the B2102. Cross and take the lane opposite. When it forks, bear right towards **Possingworth Manor**. Go through the farm buildings and turn right as the concrete ends, going through a gate and following a clearly waymarked path, with stiles, alongside several fields and a plantation to reach a road. Turn right, cross a stream and go right again over a stile. Keep to the right side of the field beyond to reach a stile in the corner. Go over and bear half-left across the next field to return to the Blackboys Inn.

POINTS OF INTEREST:

Blackboys – A little village with an historic pub, dating from 14th century and probably a 'good pull-up for coaches', on the London to Hastings run, which went via Uckfield. Black Boys means Black or Blake's Wood.

Possingworth Manor – This manor has some magnificent wrought-iron gates, well worth a detour to see.

REFRESHMENTS:
The Blackboys Inn, Blackboys.

Maps: OS Sheets Landranger 199; Pathfinder 1289.
*Small sections of the Vanguard Way and Wealdway through fine
Sussex farmland.*
Start: At 545143, Chiddingly village car park.

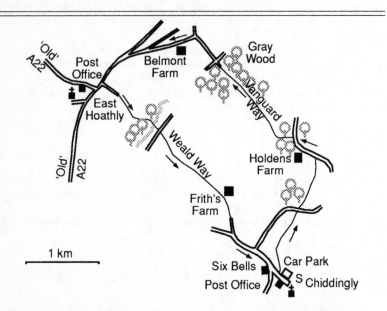

The start is in a new car park almost opposite the fine church at **Chiddingly**.

Walk back a few yards to reach the footpath opposite the Post Office. The footpath
is part of the **Vanguard Way**: keep right in the first field, go over a broken stile and
walk along the right-hand sides of two more fields. Go through a gate, to the right,
and head straight on, with a hedge now on the left, to reach a swing gate to a lane.
Turn right, along the lane, go over a stream and turn left over a stile. Now continue on
the left side of fields, using squeeze stiles between them and turning to admire the
spire of Chiddingly Church behind you. When the hedge on the left is replaced by a
fence which turns at right angles to the left, go straight ahead 50–60 yards to reach a
gap in the hedge. Go through on to a lane. Turn left along the lane, and 50 yards after
it curves right, go left along Clarklye Farm drive. After 250 yards fork right as the

verge widens. Go through a gate and follow the hedge to the left, towards a field corner. The route is now straight ahead going alongside several fields, then passing a caravan site and some woods, both to the right. Go over a chalky track and through Gray Wood. Now go through a garden to reach a lane by a house. Go directly ahead on the lane signposted for **East Hoathly** to reach the village.

In the village ignore the 'old' main A22 right turn, continuing for 200 yards to reach Buttsfield Lane, on the left. (For the church and the Foresters Arms, keep on for another 100 yards or so where they will be found to the right). Buttsfield Way is on the **Wealdway**, which is usually well waymarked with WW signs. The path is clear ahead when the lane peters out, winding through a copse, and crossing a stream, and two fields to reach a lane. Go through the gate opposite and walk to the far right-hand corner of the field beyond. Maintain the same general direction across several fields, going through gates between them, to reach a track through Frith's Farm. Follow the track as it curves right to reach a road. Ignore the left turn to Horam and, looking out for the Elizabethan ruins of Chiddingly Place now incorporated into farm buildings, to the right, follow the road back to Chiddingly.

POINTS OF INTEREST:

Chiddingly – The village church boasts a 128 foot high stone steeple and a splendid monument to Elizabeth I's Baron of Exchequer, Sir John Jefferay, in alabaster.

Vanguard Way – This long distance footpath covers 63 miles from Croydon in Surrey to Seaford in East Sussex. It has several links with the Wealdway.

East Hoathly – Until very recently, the village was on a sharp bend of the A22, London to Eastbourne, road, but a by-pass has left it a quieter village. Thomas Turner lived here (1729–1789) – a diarist, general dealer, schoolmaster and lover of drink. His recently published diary records a fascinating picture of rural life in the eighteenth century as well as details of his life with a troublesome wife(!)

The Wealdway – This excellent long distance footpath begins at Eastbourne and runs 80 miles to Gravesend.

REFRESHMENTS:

The Six Bells, Chiddingly.
The Forester's Arms, East Hoathly.
The King's Head, East Hoathly.

BATTLE AND PETLEY WOOD 6m (9$\frac{1}{2}$km)

Maps: OS sheets Landranger 199; Pathfinder 1290.

Wooded undulating countryside and a deer park.

Start: At 747162, the car park off Mount Street, Battle.

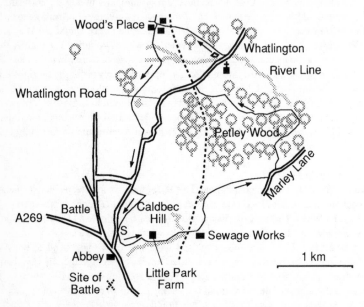

From the **Battle** car park, go over a concrete stile and then go right, down a rough lane. At the bottom, continue in an easterly direction, ignoring a footpath sign, to the right, but 50 yards further on fork right across rough ground to reach a stile and footbridge. Continue to reach another stile close to Little Park Farm which is to the left up the hill. Go over and through two fields. Now go under the railway and, keeping left of the sewage works, reach its service road. Turn left, and go uphill, on a path parallel to the railway lines. Nearing the top of the path, go over the stile ahead, and pass a barn to the right. Go through a gap and across two fields, passing under power lines. Cross another field and go over a stile to reach a road. Turn left, and as the road curves right, take the access lane, left, to Dene House. Keep ahead on this, with cottages to the right, to enter a wood.

Now bear right at a fence and then fork left into a deep track which narrows. Continue westward inside Petley Wood, going through two gates and continuing, to reach a stile. Go over and turn right, following a fence to reach a road. Turn right and follow the road passing the church, into **Whatlington**. Continue to reach Mill Lane, to the left. Take this, passing farm buildings and a wooded area, and going over the railway and on to reach Wood's Place. Go past two barns, then turn left into the farmyard and follow the sign between a barn and a storage area. Now descend, with trees to the left, to reach a sleeper bridge over a stream. Go over and turn half-left to cross a field to reach a larger bridge. Cross and ascend the hill ahead, following yellow waymarkers across the fields to reach a pond on the left. Go over a stile on the right, then go left beside a ditch and hedge. The path becomes an access road which leads to the Whatlington Road. Turn right. The road soon becomes built-up: follow it to reach a road on the right. Just beyond, opposite a grassy area also on the right, go sharp left along a lane leading to Caldbec Cottage. On reaching the cottages, go through a gate, over a stile and walk down the right edge of a field to reach a little bridge. Cross this and turn right to return to the car park.

POINTS OF INTEREST:

Battle – The battle, of course, was in 1066 (October 14th to be precise). It actually occurred just to the south of the Abbey. The altar is said to be where Harold fell. The audio-visual presentation and other attractions are very well worth adding to the pleasures of this walk (Tel: 0424-773792).

Whatlington – Look out for the Thatched Cottage, a small, listed, timber-framed homestead with an unusual verandah and arched windows. If you go into the church you will enter via the bell-tower, which could be awkward if you are early for the service!

REFRESHMENTS:

All tastes and pockets are catered for in Battle.

Walk 44   **GROOMBRIDGE**   6m (9½km)

Maps: OS Sheets Landranger 188; Pathfinder 1248.

Wooded, undulating farmland and a stretch of the Border Path.

Start: At 534365, a car park south-east of Groombridge.

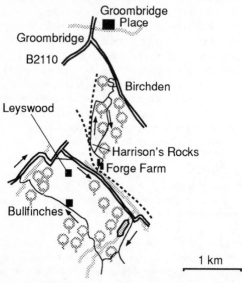

The walk begins in the car park in Aytton's Wood near Birchden, to the south-east of
Groombridge. Walk back a few yards towards the road and turn right through a gate
on to a sandy track going uphill. The path continues along the top of Harrison's Rocks,
where climbers can often be seen – potential Alpine and Himalayan adventurers! The
walk's general direction is southerly, but soon swings south-east, going out of the
wood. Go through a gate, over a stile and along a pleasant path down to Forge Farm.
Turn left at the Oast House, and cross a level crossing and a river to reach a road. Turn
left along the road to reach The Lodge. Turn right on to a path. Just past the third
house this path becomes hemmed in, with a lake to the right, and then crosses a field
to reach a bridleway in the corner. Keep straight on – a reassuring green 'Border Path'
logo should be spotted as well as a yellow waymark – then go downhill and turn right.
Cross a stile and continue north-easterly to reach a cross track. Go straight over,

heading for the corner of a wood. Walk with the trees on the left, then go over a footbridge and across fields to reach 'Bullfinches' to the right. Maintaining the same direction and following the green markers, you will soon descend to a corner of Rocks Wood.

Cross a stream and take a footpath steeply up to reach a stile. Go over on to a lane. Turn right and follow the lane for 400 yards to reach Mott's Mill. Continue uphill along the lane, swinging right and, later, left, and passing the entrance to Leyswood. About 150 yards beyond this, go over a metal stile on the right. Go diagonally across the field beyond to reach another stile in the hedge. Go over this into the next field. The Rocks are in view again, now as you cross the field and go down a lane back towards Forge Farm.

Go over the level crossing again, but now keep left at the Oast House and go through the fields with the railway immediately on the left. When the path reaches Aytton's Wood, turn right (following the yellow marker) into the trees. Very soon after bear left and follow the path back to the starting car park.

POINTS OF INTEREST:

Groombridge – although not actually on this walk, it is worth visiting the village to take in a riverside stroll to Groombridge Place, a moated mansion with peacocks and splendid grounds landscaped by the diarist John Evelyn. The village is also interesting for having the Kent-Sussex border running through it.

REFRESHMENTS:

The Crown, Groombridge.
There are also other possibilities in Groombridge, but none actually en route.

Walk 45   **BLACKBOYS AND FRAMFIELD**   6m (9½km)

Maps: OS Sheets Landranger 199; Pathfinder 1248 and 1269.

Many stiles but a gentle 'woods and fields' walk near Uckfield.

Start: At 522204, the Blackboys Inn.

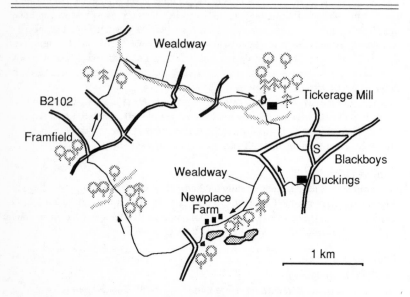

The inn is on the B2192, off the B2102, Heathfield to Uckfield road.

From the inn, in **Blackboys**, go south for 200 yards then turn right into the drive
to Duckings. Pass in front of the house and continue to reach a lane. After a further
250 yards go over a stile on the left, and follow a hedge and a fence to the corner of a
wood. You are now on a section of the **Wealdway**. Go over another stile by a gate
and turn right through a plantation and wood to reach Newplace Farm. Turn left down
the drive, going past a lake and out to a road. Turn right, but at once go left, through
a gate. Now walk with a stream, on the left, going alongside three fields, then turning
right to go up to the top left field corner. The route now continues northwards, going
over stiles, through a copse and then diagonally across a field. Go through a gate in
the next field corner and keep right in the next field to go over a stile. Go through a

little wood and then fork left across fields to reach the churchyard, and then the village, of **Framfield**.

To continue, follow the B2102 eastward and, just short of the telephone kiosk, go northwards across the recreation ground. Go over a stile and cross the field beyond to the right of the electricity poles. Now, keeping a pond in the trees to your left, go ahead through the field ahead and ascend to pass a bungalow and reach a lane. Turn left, and then right into a drive with hedges on both sides. In the field ahead, go half-left and down, to reach the next field. Go across this to reach a stile. Go over into trees, maintaining direction through them for 350 yards and then crossing a stile, into a field. Walk down to reach a stream and turn right. The route is now on the Wealdway again. Stay close to the stream through two fields, then cross a footbridge and bear right a little, to cross two more fields to reach a lane. Go across the lane and through a farmyard. Now go along the right edge of two fields, then follow the Wealdway signsthrough several more fields to reach Tickerage Mill. Turn right over the dam and sluice and go along a driveway to reach the B2102. Turn left for 150 yards, then go half-right through a gate and follow a path across the Blackboys recreation ground, to reach School Lane and the Blackboys Inn.

POINTS OF INTEREST:

Blackboys – A little village with an historic pub, dating from 14th century and probably a 'good pull-up for coaches', on the London to Hastings run, which went via Uckfield. Black Boys means Black or Blake's Wood.

The Wealdway – This excellent long distance footpath begins at Eastbourne and runs 80 miles to Gravesend.

Framfield – The 'village square' contains a good selection of architectural styles of home-building. 'Beckets' dates back to the 15th century. The church has a beautiful, modern stained-glass window depicting children at play as well as an unusual 'squint' built to allow a section of the congregation at the far southern end to view the priest saying Mass.

REFRESHMENTS:
The Blackboys Inn, Blackboys.
The Hare and Hounds, Framfield.

Walk 46   BROAD OAK AND PUNNETT'S TOWN   6m (9½km)

Maps: OS Sheets Landranger 199; Pathfinder 1270.

A walk through the woods of the Dudwell Valley. The walk can sometimes be muddy.

Start: At 606228, north of Broad Oak, off the A265.

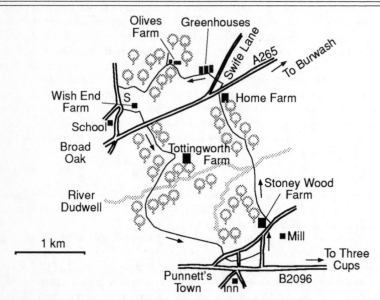

The walk starts in Street End Lane, near the drive to Wish End Farm. Go over a stile in the hedge beside the drive and head south-eastwards to reach a second stile. Go over on to the busy A265. Cross with great care and go up the drive opposite. About 100 yards past a double oast conversion, go up a bank and over a stile. Now follow a tree-lined path down to a stream. Go over the left-hand footbridge and climb up, following waymarks and curving gently left, to go through a narrow belt of trees. Go over a stile, turn sharp left and go along the left edge of a field. Gates, stiles and waymarks now guide you downhill to a wood. Turn right along the right edge of the field, heading more southerly now, to reach a crossing lane. Turn left and take the first turn right to reach The Barley Mow at **Punnett's Town**.

From the pub go north for 200 yards and turn right opposite a garage to go along the right edge of a field to reach a lane. Turn left. Do not turn right at the next junction (which leads to the mill): instead, bear right with the lane. Another lane comes in from the left: soon after, turn up left using an access drive to Storey Wood Farm. Ignore a left turn, but continue ahead, downhill through the woods, as waymarked. About $^3/_4$ mile ($1^1/_4$kms) after the farm you will reach a footbridge over the river. Cross and walk uphill on a very pleasant path with trees, and then a fence, to the right. Now follow an access drive to reach the A265 near Home Farm.

Go right then cross the main road with care and go left over a stile. Cross the field beyond to reach Swife Lane. Cross the lane to the track opposite. At a fork, bear left and go past some greenhouses, to the right. The path narrows and descends to reach a plank bridge. Cross, walk past a Tennis Court and cross a second footbridge. Now follow waymarks through woodland and across a field, and go through the buildings of Olives Farm. Cross a stile at a corner by a barn. Beyond, where the main drive goes left, keep straight on to walk through Black Sand Wood. Continue, to reach a lane north of Broad Oak. Turn left and follow the lane back to the start.

POINTS OF INTEREST:

Punnett's Town – The *white* smockmill, which once stood among cherry orchards, has been lovingly restored. Kipling (who lived and worked at Bateman's in nearby Burwash) mentions the mill in many of his writings, calling it Cherry *Black*. Its real name is Cherry Clack but it was/is sometimes called Blackdown Mill. Is all that clear!

REFRESHMENTS:

The Barley Mow, Punnett's Town.
The Star Inn, Old Heathfield (not en route).

Walk 47   **CROWHURST**   6m (9¹/₂km)

Maps: OS Sheets Landranger 199; Pathfinder 1290.

Field paths and an RSPB *reserve.*

Start: At 760129, Crowhurst Railway Station.

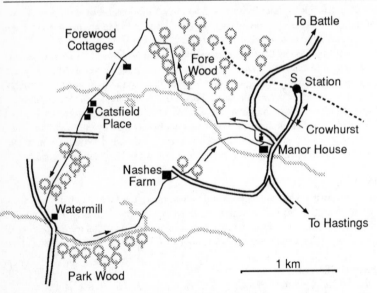

Walk south from the station and turn right into **Crowhurst** churchyard. Keep left and leave through a gate on to a lane. Turn left, and just before a telephone kiosk go left over a stile by a gate. Go along the right edge of a field, then forward across the next field to reach a path between banks. Now go right a little and cross a field to reach a wood near a Nature Reserve sign. Continue along the woodland path, past a pond to the left. Go out of the wood through a gap by the railings and swing northwards and then right to reach another wood. When an empty cottage is reached, turn left (facing it) to go along a drive which curves gently left and right, then descends and ascends, roughens, and passes Catsfield Place. At a junction of paths keep right with the drive, following it to a lane.

Cross the lane and take the track just to the right of a drive, walking half-right across the field ahead to reach a stile. Go over – it might be rickety – and descend

96

with a fence and bank to the left. We now make for the corner of the small wood ahead, as waymarked and keeping it to the left, go over a stile. Go under power lines and along a woodland path to emerge on a lane by Watermill.

Turn left along the lane and, after passing Rose Cottage, go left over a low wall, using the gate and steps. Follow the narrow path beyond over a footbridge and across the bottom of several fields with the stream on your right. After about $^1/_2$ mile ($^3/_4$kms) cross a ditch (a little to the left) and go back down to the stream. Cross on a little bridge and head for a gate in front of a pylon. Do not go through: instead, turn right down a slope, go left through a gate and then climb up again. Go under the power lines and make for the buildings ahead. Go through a gate and continue to Nashes Farm, passing a barn, to the left, to reach a concrete drive. Follow this to a lane. Turn right and, shortly after, go left through a gate. Go downhill and cross several fields, going over fences and through three gates, to reach Powdermill Stream. Cross and bear right, making directly for the churchyard where the walk began.

POINTS OF INTEREST:

Crowhurst – The artist J. M. W. Turner worked in this area, setting several paintings locally. Just south of the church there are the ruins of a 13th century manor, and there is evidence of much earlier, Roman, occupation hereabouts too. The church tower dates from 1450, the rest having been rebuilt in 1857. The nearby yew is very ancient, and has a girth of more than 40 feet. It was probably growing when William landed from Normandy and defeated Harold at nearby Battle.

REFRESHMENTS:

Available in nearby Battle.

Walk 48 COODEN BEACH AND NORMAN'S BAY 6m (9½m)

Maps: OS Sheets Landranger 199; Pathfinder 1309.

A flat walk across levels, which can be muddy, and along the beach.

Start: At 711066, Cooden Beach car park in 'The Gorses'.

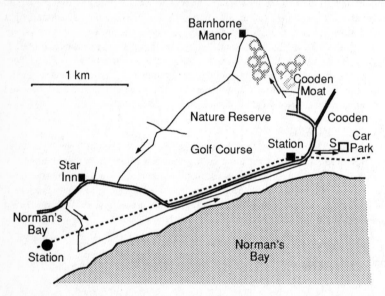

Turn left out of the car park and then go right, walking away from the sea along Cooden Sea Road. Go past the golf course club-house, to the left, and then turn left into Clavering Walk. Next, go right into Maple Walk. Now turn left along the track beside 'Friars Charm' to reach a stile and gate. Go over the stile into a field and, keeping the hedge on your right, walk along and enter a wood. Cross a stream and a stile into a field, and maintain direction, with the wood to the left, to reach another stile with Barnhorne Manor to the right. Go over and follow a path as it swings west and then south. Continue to reach a stile by a footpath sign. Follow the path signed for Norman's Bay, keeping a hedge on your right. Go over several more stiles, following the well-signed path. Soon you will come to a signpost by some trees on a little hill.

Despite the hill being a mere 40 feet above sea level, the views are extensive over the surrounding, flat landscape.

Obey the signpost yet again, going into a field and walking with a ditch and hedge to the left, to reach a bridge. Cross the bridge to reach marshy land and continue, still with a hedge and a ditch to the left. Go under telephone lines to reach a gate leading into another field. Cross to the stile ahead. Go over to reach a bridge on the left and another bridge ahead. Do not take the one leading on to the golf course: instead go over the one ahead and, keeping a wide ditch on your left, go on diagonally across a field. Now go through several gates and over a stile on to a road. Turn right for about 400 yards, to reach the Star Inn, on the right. Continue along the road for a further 80–100 yards, then take a footpath to the left. Cross a railway line, with care, then turn right to reach a little brick building by some pylons. Turn left and walk past houses and shops, continuing down to reach the beach at **Norman's Bay**. The route now simply goes along the beach for 2 miles (3kms) the walker enjoying the view and sound of the sea, and the sea-birds. Just past Cooden Beach Station leave the beach by going left up to the Sea Road and return to the start.

POINTS OF INTEREST:

Quiet walkers should see many sea and marsh birds. The route passes through the levels, marshland and along the seashore, a real mix of habitats.

Norman's Bay – Today, the bay named for invaders who landed nine centuries ago is a quiet caravan and camping resort where swimming, sailing and surfing can be enjoyed.

REFRESHMENTS:

The Star Inn, Norman's Bay.
The Harrow Inn, Cooden (and others).

Walk 49 NORTH-EAST HASTINGS AND PETT 6m (9¹/₂km)

Maps: OS Sheets Landranger 199; Pathfinder 1291.

A walk over delightfully, undulating countryside.

Start: At 848115, the large car park on Fairlight Road, Hastings.

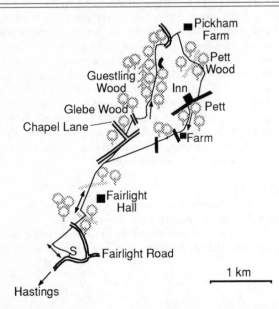

Leave the car park and turn right for a few yards to enter a field via a kissing-gate and a signpost! Turn left along a field edge, go through two more gates and then bear right, downhill to reach a road. Cross and go over the stile ahead (not along the lane). After walking 300 yards, by a stile in the trees to the right, turn left across the field to the hedge and turn right there to go downhill. Go through a gap on the left before reaching the bottom of the field, and cross a field, going under power lines to reach a footpath sign at the edge of a wood. Follow the sign, entering the wood and going down to cross two bridges before emerging from the trees into a small steep field. Go straight across to reach a stile. Go over, and cross the lane beyond to reach another stile. Go over and on to a third stile. The path beyond may be too discernible, so carefully bear left uphill towards some trees and a hidden pond. Now go left through a gap. Go to the left of marshy ground and walk on to reach the busy Pett Road. Go right, downhill, and then turn left into Chapel Lane. Almost at once follow the signed concrete footpath to the right, going up into Glebe Wood. Maintain direction, with open fields to the right, for 600 yards to cross into Church Lane by a thatched cottage. Go up the stone steps by another concrete marker and follow a track. The track becomes a tarmac lane: follow it as it turns left towards some houses. Turn right (there is a sign, but it might be hidden by hedges) and go through a kissing-gate into a field. Keep by the hedge on the left, and after 50 yards go left through a metal gate just short of a stone garage. Follow the gravel path beyond, going past 'Shellies' cottages.

Go through the left-hand of two gates and then ahead along the left side of several fields to reach Guestling Wood. Carefully now, go straight into the wood for 30 yards, go right for 20 yards, then left on a narrow, but clear, path, going downhill for another 200 yards. The wood becomes more open: by a prominently raised manhole cover, turn right for about 10 yards, then left into a narrow track that leads uphill. A further 200 yards now brings you to a lane corner by a gate. Do not leave the wood: instead, go forward into a less-wooded area, for another 150–200 yards. At a junction of tracks by some oak trees, go right, through a hurdle gate, into a field. Cross the field corner to emerge on to a lane. Turn left and walk to a sharp left bend, and go ahead there on to the concrete lane leading to Pickham Farm. About 150 yards down this lane, just before a modern house on the left, go right over a stile in a hedge (the stile is often obscured) and climb up by the fence on the left. Maintaining direction, enter Pett Wood ahead by way of a gate or stile. In the wood go downhill, cross a stream and go up to a wire fence. Turn right and follow the fence to reach a stile. Go over on to a track and follow it to another stile. Turn right, then left by a pond (on the left). Now follow the hedge on the left, going down by a garden and then following an enclosed path to reach a gravelly drive. Follow this to reach a stile just to the left of French Court Farm. 'The Barn' is opposite: keep ahead (actually slightly left) along the drive to reach the road in Pett, opposite a garage. Turn right to reach the Two Sawyers Inn, on the right. A few yards on, but across the road on the left, take a footpath going downhill through woods. On emerging, cross the field ahead, go to the right of a farm and over a stile on to Rosemary Lane. Cross the lane and go over a stile. Go through more fields, heading westward, to reach Peter James Lane. Cross, and go ahead across more fields. Now go up a bank, cross several more stiles and, with the masts near the walk's start appearing, keep ahead through trees. The way should be familiar now, take a look back at the magnificent view and retrace the outward route back to the start.

REFRESHMENTS:
The Two Sawyers Inn, Pett.
There are also numerous opportunities, for all possible tastes, in Hastings.

Walk 50　　**ALL AROUND NINFIELD**　　6m (9¹/₂km)

Maps: OS Sheets Landranger 199; Pathfinder 1290.

Field paths and woodland walks around a village north of Bexhill.

Start: At 705123, Ninfield Church.

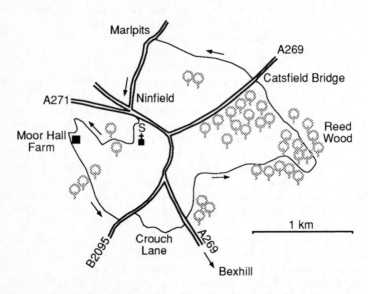

Leave the churchyard in **Ninfield** through a white gate and turn left. Go over a stile and descend, westwards, for 200 yards to reach a bridge. Cross and go into the little wood ahead. On emerging from the wood, keep left across a field to reach a gate and stile. Go over and walk uphill to reach another stile in a wooden fence. Go over and cross the field beyond to its far left corner to reach a lane. Turn left for about 100 yards, then, go right along a farm access lane. Go through the farm (Moor Hall Farm) and as the lane bends right, go straight on and down to reach a stream. Cross the stream and fork right. Then, with a fence to the right, walk forward to reach a stile. Go over and maintain the south-easterly direction along a green lane to reach some farm buildings. Turn right here and walk to the B2095. Turn left, go along the road, with care. After 200 yards, turn right into the quieter Crouch Lane, following it to reach the A269. Turn left along it, with even more care, and after 120 yards go right along an enclosed path, heading north-eastwards. Go over several stiles and to the right of the power lines to reach the left field corner. Go over the stile there, and veer right between a pair of ponds at Ingram's Farm.

Continue in a more easterly direction, going over stiles and then downhill towards woodland. At the bottom, keep left to go between two woods. Further down, keep to a track between Sprays Wood, on the right, and more open land, to the left. Walk to a point 20 yards short of the power line poles and then go left, with a stream on the right. Soon, cross the stream by a footbridge and turn right along the edge of Reed Wood, making for a large electricity substation. Short of the station's boundary fence, by a pylon, turn left for 200 yards, then go left again by another pylon, into a wood. Maintain direction, ignoring all cross-paths for $^3/_4$ mile ($1^1/_2$kms), to reach an access drive. Follow the drive to reach the A269 at Catsfield Bridge. Cross the road carefully and go along the track opposite towards Marlpits. Go through two gates, pass a pond, on the left, and go over several stiles to reach a lane. Turn left here and soon go left again, following the lane back to Ninfield village and the start of the walk.

POINTS OF INTEREST:
Ninfield – The church of St Mary the Virgin has some medieval parts, but was much 'restored' in Victorian days. The clock inside is rather special, brassy, blue and busily thumping. Near the church, in High Street, be sure to find, and ponder over the stocks and whipping-post. The stocks are of iron, not wood, holes for ankles and four wrist-clamps – you had little chance of escaping your punishment if you were sentenced to remain in these for a spell.

REFRESHMENTS:
The United Friends Inn, Ninfield.

SEAFORD

Maps: OS Sheets Landranger 199; Pathfinder 1324.
River bank, clifftops and downland.
Start: At 492987, the Southdown Road/Chyngton Road junction,
Seaford.

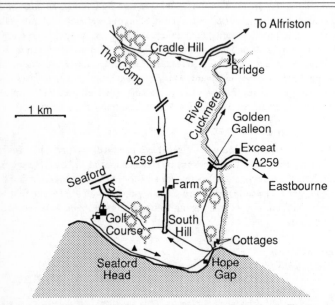

This walk takes in Seaford's clifftops and the Cuckmere river bank. The longer option
adds splendid downland. Choose a clear day to appreciate the views fully.

Walk southwards up Southdown Road to reach the Golf Club House. Just before
the entrance, turn right and cross rough ground with houses, right, and the 18th green,
left, to reach a clear path going left (eastwards) and uphill. The cliff edge is not without
danger but offers views to Brighton and beyond: it is possible to see Selsey Bill and
the Isle of Wight in very clear conditions. Keep to the path as it passes tumuli and the
early British camp at Seaford Head (only 275 feet, though it seems higher if you have
just climbed it!). Now descend into Cliff Bottom, a deep valley dropping to steps at
Hope Gap, about a mile from the Head. (A fine detour here would be to descend the

steps and to walk eastwards along the seashore for $^1/_2$ mile, going below the cliff and coast-guard cottages and then going left up the beach, but <u>only</u> if the tide is low or ebbing.) From the top of the steps the cliff path goes steeply uphill and a little inland: keep well away from the edge but enjoy the view of the Seven Sisters and Cuckmere Haven ahead. Go over a cattle grid, then downhill to the beach, passing the Coastguard cottages to reach the mouth of the Cuckmere river. Now go left, inland and head north along the **Straight Cut** of the River, on the right. After about a mile, leave the river, turning left for 50 often muddy yards to reach a cross-path. The Golden Galleon Inn is 150 yards to the right here.

For the shorter walk, turn left over the stile into the Nature Reserve and head southwards, going over stiles, to a point about 200 yards short of the Coastguard cottages. Here go uphill, half-right, to reach a stile. Cross to turn right, ascending, past wooden seats (if you sit on one you might 'slide down the banisters'!) to reach a cattle grid. Maintain direction to reach a car park at South Hill. Keep walking westward, not on the concrete path but alongside the field, to the right, to reach the 13th green of the golf course. Now go half-right, downhill, through bushes. The track crosses the golf course, so beware of golfers and balls as you descend back to the start.

For the longer walk, do not cross the stile, but turn right to reach the Golden Galleon's car park. Go ahead to the A259. Cross, with care, and turn right over a bridge. Immediately beyond, cross a stile on the left to reach the right bank of the River Cuckmere. Follow this for $1^1/_2$ miles ($2^1/_2$ kms) to reach a bridge. Cross the bridge and go steeply uphill, veering left. At a stile in the hedge to the right, cross on to a busy road. Cross the road and go through the gate opposite to reach a downland valley (Cradle Hill). Walk along the valley, there are primroses galore in season, to reach a track going half-left uphill to the Comp. There turn sharp left on to a track back towards Seaford. Follow the track to reach the Alfriston road. Cross and maintain a southerly course along an enclosed path to reach the A259. Cross, with care, into a lane and follow it to a concrete road that leads to South Hill car park. Turn right, rejoining the short walk and following it back to the start.

POINTS OF INTEREST:

The Straight Cut – The Cut was made in 1846 to prevent flooding of the Cuckmere Valley. There is an automatic weir control.

REFRESHMENTS:

The Golden Galleon, Exceat.

There are also several possibilities in Seaford.

Walk 53 COOKSBRIDGE AND BARCOMBE MILLS 6m (9¹/₂km)

Maps: OS Sheets Landranger 198; Pathfinder 1289.

Fieldpath walking from just north of Lewes to Barcombe Mills.

Start: At 403143, the Rainbow Inn, on the A275, north of Lewes.

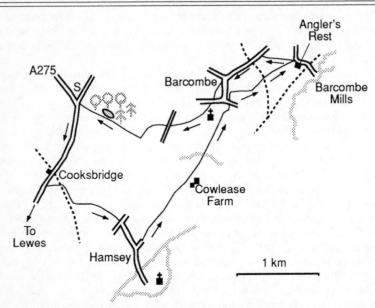

Walk down the main road from the Rainbow Inn to reach the railway station in Cooksbridge, heading towards Lewes. About 300 yards further on, turn left on to a concrete drive by Nursery Cottage and then go left through a gate by a garage. Take the footpath running beside a ditch, then go over a stile and cross the field beyond to reach another stile. Go over and walk straight ahead, taking special care, of course!, as you go over the railway line. Now turn right, walking alongside the line and passing two fields, to the left, to reach a gap in a hedge. Go through and turn left along the hedge. At the corner, go right for about 20 yards, then left through another gap. Cross the field ahead to reach a stile. Go over to reach Hamsey Lane. Turn right, but at once go left, maintaining the original direction and heading towards the distant **Hamsey** Church. After 400 yards turn left along an old track to reach Cowlease Farm, passing the buildings on your right.

Maintain direction to pass Apple Cottage. Beyond, go up a road, along a narrow footpath and then across a field, bearing half-right to reach a footbridge, with trees over to the left. Cross the bridge and walk ahead to go over the old railway line. Continue to a stile, going over it and a footbridge. Go through a gate and continue to reach the busy and sometimes hazardous road just to the left of the Anglers Rest Inn. To continue, turn left along the road, for a few yards only, to reach a the sharp right-hand bend, and a stile, to the left. Cross this and go straight ahead (not half-right!) to the far corner of the field. Go over into Church Road. Turn left, following the road over the railway again. Keep right at a lane junction, but almost immediately go left, through a gate. Keep to the fence on your left, crossing the field and going out through another gate on to a road by **Barcombe** Church. Go over to the church and along the path to the right of the porch to reach the cemetery. Go through to reach a field at the rear. Now head for the left end of a wooded area on the far side of two fields where a barn will be seen on the right. Pass the barn on your right to emerge on to a lane. Cross over and go through the gateway opposite. Go straight across the field beyond to reach a track. Follow this westwards, passing farm buildings, a pond and some conifers to reach the A275 at the 'end of the Rainbow'!

POINTS OF INTEREST:

Hamsey – A tiny hamlet now, with a church dedicated to St Peter, isolated and locked (key available from Hamsey Place Farm) and the haunt of kingfishers. Yet it was once important enough for the Saxon King Athelstan to hold a council meeting here in 925 AD. It is assumed that the population was wiped out by plague in the 17th century.

Barcombe – St Mary's Church has 11th century origins and an interesting, modern, glass memorial screen.

REFRESHMENTS:

The Rainbow Inn, Cooksbridge.
The Royal Oak, Barcombe (There is Maypole Dancing here on May Day).
The Angler's Rest, Barcombe Mills.

Maps: OS Sheets Landranger 199; Pathfinder 1271.

A gentle walk through fields near the Kent border.

Start: At 823223, Horns Cross, on the A28 north of Hastings.

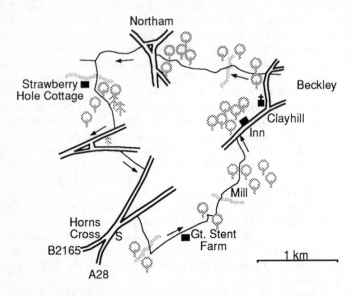

From the junction of the A28 and B2165 at Horns Cross, about 7 miles north of Hastings, go north-eastwards along the B2165 and, about 125 yards from the village edge, go through a metal gate on the right. Take the path along the left hedge, walking past oast houses, then over a hill and down to a gate. Maintain direction, going under power lines to reach a stile and footbridge. Cross and ascend the field beyond towards a clump of trees. Go through a hedge-gap and turn sharp left along the hedge on the left. Pass two gates but go through a third into the next field. Keep to the left hedge again and make for Great Stent Farm. Go through a metal gate, turn right, then left along the farm's drive crossing a triangle of grass between the buildings. Beyond them, turn right, beside a gate, into a field. Walk with hedges to the left, going over two stiles and skirting left around a field to reach a third stile. Cross and go ahead to pass a copse and a rubbish dump. Cross a footbridge over a stream, then walk past huts and a splendid water mill. Go through a gate and walk to a drive. Turn right, go through another gate, pass a chicken farm and cross a stile. Turn left along the field edge. Turn right at a signpost, walk along a field edge, and go over a stile on to a drive. Go half-left, taking the middle path into a wood. On reaching the wood's far edge, turn right, but shortly go left to a field corner. Go up this field to the top left corner. Go through a gap, bear right on to a drive and follow it to the road at Clayhill. Turn right, keep right at the junction, walk past the Rose and Crown Inn and, at the next junction, go left to pass **Beckley Church**. About 400 yards further along Stoddards Lane, turn left along a fenced footpath for 50 yards, then go over a stile and walk along a section of the Sussex Border Path. Pass through a little wood, crossing stiles and a footbridge, then go diagonally across a field into another wooded area. Now go gently uphill, with Northiam Church clearly ahead. Walk under power lines to reach a gap in trees. Go through a gate and along a fence in front of some houses. Go through a second gate and into a lane, to descend it to the main road and the Six Bells Inn, **Northiam**. Turn right and after 400 yards, pick up the Border Path again to reach a gate marked 'Westwell'. Follow the path to 'Mill Corner' and 'Ewhurst', crossing a stile and a footbridge en route. At the next stile, do not go over: instead, turn left before it (there is another sign for Mill Corner) and descend to cross another stile and bridge, with Strawberry Hole Cottage oast on your right. Now head southwards, going up and through Gusling Wood. At its end, turn left (yet another post to Mill Corner) and ascend, with the wood on your left, towards houses, reaching a road at Yew Tree Cottage. Turn right along the road, going left by Copper Cottage. After 100 yards, turn left again by Pippins, and after another 400 yards go right through a gate. Now go half-left down the valley to emerge on to the A28. Turn right and follow the road, with care, back to Horns Cross.

POINTS OF INTEREST:
Beckley Church – All Saints Church has an 11th century spire and a 15th century east window, fascinating, grotesque corbels and a dug-out chest, banded with iron, to keep ecclesiastical treasures in.

Northiam – Walkers with an interest in old houses should not miss Great Dixter (15th century timber-frame plus gardens, Tel: 0797 2531690) or Brickwall (with topiary chess garden etc, Tel: 0797 223329).

REFRESHMENTS:
The Rose and Crown, Clayhill.
The Six Bells, Northiam.

Walk 55 BERWICK AND CHARLESTON FARMHOUSE 6m (9¹/₂km)
Maps: OS Sheets Landranger 199; Pathfinder 1308.
Bloomsbury painters and two rather special Sussex churches.
Start: At 505054, in Alciston.

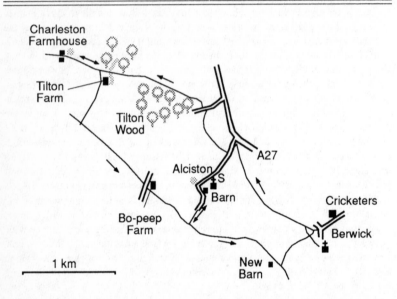

A short walk, but three stops to visit the Places of Interest are essential and will add hours to the overall time.

Walk down the village street, past the Rose Cottage Inn and detour to see church. Return to the lane, walk around the great tithe barn and go past the 30 mph sign, heading towards the South Downs. Some 200 yards further on you will meet the ancient **Coach Road**, a wide track: turn left (eastwards) walking through open fields to reach New Barn, to the right. Shortly beyond the barn there is a junction where the old road enters woodland. Turn left here, following the waymarks and, eventually, going uphill to join a track between farm buildings. This track soon bends right to reach a junction of lanes. Turn left here to reach the Cricketers Inn, though a right turn to visit the church of **St Michael and All Angels, Berwick** is also essential.

To continue the walk return to the junction and retrace your steps a few yards. Now go ahead, not left, to pass in front of farm cottages, heading westward. Go alongside the left edges of three fields and then cross three more fields using double stiles and plank bridges. The crossing of the last field takes you towards the main road, but look for a 'twitten' and stile between houses before the corner is reached: this will lead you out to the lane in Alciston near the starting point. Turn left, but almost at once turn right on to the path opposite, following it across two fields and along the right edge of a third field to emerge into a lane.

Go left along the lane, but very soon turn right along a clear track, maintaining the general westerly direction. After $^3/_4$ mile you will arrive at a little copse and stream where stout boots (and a stout heart) may be necessary to get out to the far side. Once over, walk towards the buildings of Tilton Farm. The route is clear now, reaching a junction of tracks. Note, but do not take the southerly track which heads towards the Downs, continue ahead (westward) to reach **Charleston Farmhouse**. After a visit, retrace the route back to the junction and turn right, to go along the track towards the Downs. Follow this track to reach the old Coach Road again. Turn left and follow the old road for a mile, passing Bo-peep Farm to reach a junction passed earlier on the walk. Now turn left to return to the starting point in **Alciston**.

POINTS OF INTEREST:

Coach Road – This was once the main road from Hastings to Lewes.

St Michael and All Angels, Berwick – Spare at least half an hour to visit the church which has murals painted, in the Forties, by members of the 'Bloomsbury Group'. Note especially the many Sussex features – trug baskets, sheep and shepherd, the typical barn, Mount Caburn etc. Note, too, that the angels have Forties hair-dos and that the kneeling figures are uniformed servicemen.

Charleston Farmhouse – This is a 'decorated house', with painted furniture, ceramics, textiles and murals, mostly the work of the 'Bloomsbury' artists who lived here from 1916 until the 1970's. (Tel: 0323 811265).

Alciston – Note the fine timbered and thatched cottages, the part-Norman church with its fishy weathervane, the medieval dovecote and the large tithe barn.

REFRESHMENTS:

The Rose Cottage Inn, Alciston.
The Cricketers Inn, Berwick.
Teas are sometimes available at Charlestown Farmhouse.

Walk 56   FLIMWELL AND BEWL WATER   6m (9½km)

Maps: OS Sheets Landranger 188; Pathfinder 1249.

A reservoir and woodland walk on the Kent/Sussex border.

Start: At 711321, the car park and picnic site on the A21.

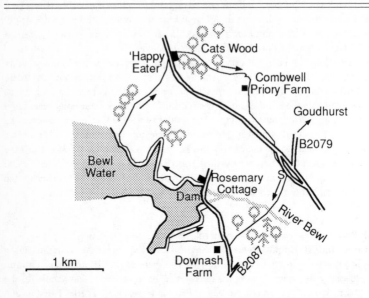

The walk is on an old section of the A21 about ½ mile north of Flimwell. Head north-west and parallel to the A21, to your right, towards a post box in a brick pillar. Just before reaching this, take a path to the left. Soon, the path bears left beside a garden and then goes half-right across a big field. Go past several large trees, then descend to reach a footbridge (over the River Bewl) and stile. Cross and enter a wood along a narrow path. Now climb up, heading south-westward, but soon descend again, ignoring a cross-track. The wood is a fine mixture of silver birch and conifers: on reaching a 'Private Woodland' sign, the path bears left. Do not follow it: instead, go ahead over a stile and walk through pasture and a rough area to reach a lane. Turn right along the lane for about 150 yards, then go half-left (due west) along a concrete bridleway. Soon the concrete becomes a dirt path: continue through gates and alongside three fields, to the right, then descend to reach the perimeter path of **Bewl Water**.

Turn right and follow the water's edge closely for $^1/_2$ mile to reach a road. Turn left along the road and cross the dam. About 50 yards beyond the dam, go left along an access drive, passing Rosemary Cottage, and then going alongside the water again. Follow the water for a mile or so, then cross a stile on the right, by a 'Post Boy' sign. Climb up, passing between a bank and a tall fence, and continuing to reach an access drive. Continue past a converted oast-house to reach the A21. Turn left along the A21 (a very busy road so care is needed) towards 'The Happy Eater café' but 50 yards short of it, enter Cats Wood on the right.

The easterly path through the wood is clear at first, but care is needed after about 300 yards – look out for the yellow arrows, on the trees, marking the way. On reaching a footbridge and stile at the wood's edge, go forward and a little right to reach a hedge, to the right. Follow this hedge to reach a stile and gate. Cross and ascend a little hill (a yellow waymark confirms) continuing towards a house. In a dip, take a track through trees and, with farm buildings to the right, continue until the path turns right (south) with Combwell Priory Farm to the left. Now follow the farm's access drive, but as it swings right towards the main road, go through a gate on the left to reach a stile in the hedge just to the right of a stone shed. Go over and head south-eastwards, going over stiles and along a hedge to reach the A21. With the usual care, cross both carriageways to find the old road where the walk began.

POINTS OF INTEREST:

Bewl Water – The reservoir was formed by flooding 770 acres of land in the early seventies. It is now a mecca for fly fishers, bird watchers, water sportsmen, riders and walkers. There's a children's playground, a passenger boat (summer time cruises) and many attractions to 'make a day of it'. For information Tel: 0892 890661.

REFRESHMENTS:

The Post Boy on the A21.
The Happy Eater café on the A21.
Bewl Water's Visitors Centre.

Walks 57 & 58   **THE CUCKMERE VALLEY**   6¹/₂m (10¹/₂km)
or 9m (14¹/₂km)

Maps: OS Sheets Landranger 199; Pathfinder 1324.
A varied walk through the Cuckmere Valley as it meets the sea.
Start: At 502005, a lay-by on Alfriston Road, north of Seaford.

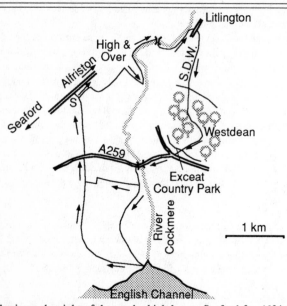

The lay-by is on the right of the road which leaves Seaford for Alfriston. Walk on towards Alfriston for a few yards and then turn right past the hedge. As the path enters a 'twitten' between hedges, turn left and go up a field with a hedge to your right. Follow the hedge as it turns sharp right and on to reach a gate and stile. Go over and turn left at once to walk along the fence (and, later, a hedge), going over stiles to reach the sharp crest of **High and Over**. The route descends the steep crest by turning right, but first turn up left to reach an information table and picnic area, and to enjoy the view. Now descend the clear path ahead with great care, occasionally using rough steps. Turn left at the valley floor and walk to the river bank. Go over a stile and, at a bridge, cross and turn left over a stile. Continue in same direction, but with the river now on your left. Just before a white bridge, leave the bank and go right to an iron gate on to a road. Turn left and go around two curves at the entrance to Litlington Village. For refreshments go straight on to the pub, on the left and the tearoom. At the 'Private Road' turn right into it and then go right going through a kissing-gate.

You are now on the South Downs Way (with its acorn way-marks). Follow the telephone lines uphill to the left corner of a field and go over two stiles. Continue along the right side of fields and then descend fairly steeply to reach a stile. Follow the acorn way-marks left, then round to the right and, as the wood closes in, climb steps at a signpost. Go over a stile at the top and continue along a wide path. Keep to the acorn-marked Way, ignoring all crossing paths as it curves left beside Corsican pines to the left and above Westdean Village to the right. At a T-junction of paths, turn right and descend over a stile into the flint-walled village with its attractive pond. Pass the green telephone kiosk and turn right, going around the pond and forward on to a wide track. After about 400 yards the track forks: bear left and slightly uphill to reach a gate into a car park. Refreshments are available to the left at the Exceat Farmhouse. Go straight on to a gap, where the **Exceat Country Park Centre** is to the left, and along the road for 500 yards. Go over Exceat Bridge and turn left through the Golden Galleon Inn car park. At the far side of the car park is a stile: go over and on for 300 yards to reach a stile at the entrance to Seaford Head Nature Reserve.

For the shorter walk, turn right here and take the clear path between fields. Turn left and then right, between fences at the top to emerge into Chyngton Lane to re-join the longer walk.

The longer walk continues ahead, through gates and over stiles to reach the river mouth, slightly left below the Coastguard's Cottages. Go right, uphill, to a cattle grid into a car park. Turn right on to a road down to Chyngton Farm. As the road turns left at the bottom, keep straight on, through a vehicle barrier, to meet, after $^1/_4$ mile, the shorter route. Continue up the lane to reach the A259. Cross and go straight on through the hedged 'twitten' with houses to the left. Now follow this path back to the start.

POINTS OF INTEREST:

High and Over – Take the very short detour to enjoy the view and glean interesting information set out on a panoramic board.

Exceat Country Park Centre – Time should be found to visit the excellent and very informative Park Information and Exhibition Centre.

REFRESHMENTS:

The Plough & Harrow, Litlington.

The Golden Galleon Inn, Exceat Bridge.

Exceat Farmhouse at the Exhibition Centre.

Walks 59 & 60 SEVEN SISTERS AND FRISTON FOREST 6¹/₂m (10km) or 9m (14¹/₂km)

Maps: OS Sheets Landranger 199; Pathfinder 1324.
Spectacular cliff scenery and a fine forest walk.
Start: At 550979, the National Trust car park near Friston Church.

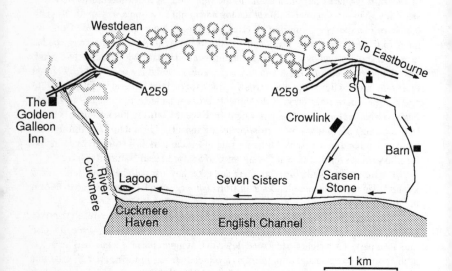

For the longer walk, having arrived at the car park from the A259, retrace your steps about 50 yards towards the pond, and go right, through a gate, into open pasture. Now aim south-south-east for a swing gate in the fence ahead. Go through and turn left, with a fence to the left, to reach another gate. Go through and on towards some trees. The field now drops away leftwards: keep to the path heading due south, making for a red-roofed barn about 400 yards distant. Keeping to the right of the barn, follow the path through gates and just short of some houses, go sharply right to pick up the clear, acorn-marked track, the South Downs Way. You are now striding along, with Birling Gap behind you, at the first of the **Seven Sisters**. Pass the monument, and evidence of a tumuli, right, and two more 'Sisters' to reach a prominent Sarsen Stone near a seat. At this point the longer route rejoins the shorter variant.

For the short walk, leave the car park walking south towards the sea. Go past a cattle grid and keep a little to the left, going up to a rise and then ahead on a clear path to reach a gate, with the hamlet of Crowlink below and to your right. Go through and continue in the same direction to reach the Sarsen Stone. Turn right here, having rejoined the longer walk.

We continue along the South Downs Way, going past the remaining four Sisters, until **Cuckmere Haven** and the cliffs of Seaford Head appear ahead (Haven Brow). The path now drops, gently at first, then steeply into a valley. Make for the path which runs to the left of a lagoon, following it to reach the river bank. Now turn right, following the river, which becomes very straight and leads to the A259 at Exceat Bridge. Turn right along the road for 500 yards to the Country Park and Information Centre (*see* Note to Walks 57 & 58). At the green telephone kiosk, cross the road and go between the last two buildings on the right. Go over a stile and uphill across a field. Cross a stone stile and look back to view the meandering Cuckmere River before going straight ahead into a wood. Take the steps downhill to reach the valley floor. There, you will turn right, but a short detour left is recommended to enjoy the pond, peace and flint walled homes of **Westdean**. From the steps turn right and continue for 2 miles (3kms) through the forest, passing a single cottage, to the left, before coming to a T-junction with a lane at another cottage and pumping station. Here, turn right uphill, for about 200 yards, then go left on a level 'shelf' in the wood. The shelf gradually ascends to reach the A259 and Friston Pond at a stone stile. Cross, with care, and go to the left of the pond and to the right of the church. Now walk straight ahead on a track that leads back to the car park.

POINTS OF INTEREST:
The Seven Sisters – There are really eight, but seven has a better 'ring'. The Sisters are chalk cliffs formed where the South Downs meet the sea. The route, follows the cliff edge: take care – rock falls are possible and unpredictable!

Cuckmere Haven – A classic example of a meandering river winding over a flat plain – the straight cut from Exceat Bridge to the sea was made in 1846. Watch out for herons, geese, shelduck and many more birds.

Westdean – Alfred the Great is reputed to have had a palace here and to have kept a fleet on the river.

REFRESHMENTS:
The Golden Galleon Inn, Exceat Bridge.

ARLINGTON RESERVOIR AND MICHELHAM PRIORY
$6^1/_2$m ($10^1/_2$km)

Maps: OS Sheets Landranger 199; Pathfinder 1308.
A walk round the reservoir and a visit to the old Priory.
Start: At 526067, Berwick Station.

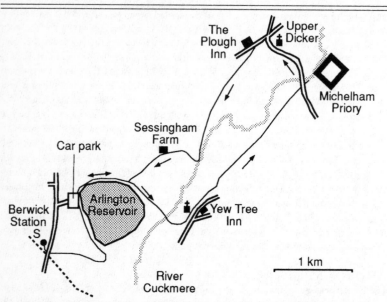

Leave the station and turn left along the road for a few yards, then turn right between a shop and a garage following a sign to the Reservoir. Cross a field to a point left of a ruined barn and cross another field to reach stiles and a footbridge. Beyond, keep to the hedge on the right, with a good view of the reservoir, and then turn left at the access road to the farm on the right. The road leads to Polhills: go carefully round, through gates to reach a road to the Reservoir's car park. Turn right towards the water, and keep left following footpath signs, with the shore on the right. When the path forks, keep right and descend towards the end of the dam. At stiles and signs, turn left, away from the dam, and head across fields on a path towards a bridge. Cross and go half-left to a field corner. Keep a ditch on your left and go through a hedge and across the next field to reach a lane with **Arlington Church** to the left. Take the kissing-

118

gate into the churchyard and with a hedge on the right, follow a path down to a footbridge. Cross the field beyond to reach a gate (to the right of a pylon) in the far right-hand corner. Walk beside trees, and then a hedge, to the right going over stiles to the lane at Raylands Farm. Go right, then left on the lane, then over a stile. Cross a small field to reach a stile in the opposite hedge. In the next field go to the right of a pylon in the far corner. There, ignore a gate: but keep the hedge on your right to reach a stile and then a gate. Cross the next field to a stile into a small copse. Follow a path over a bridge and into a field. Keep alongside the river to pass a small pumping station, then go over a stile and bridge. Cross the next field, in the same direction, going away from the river (left) towards the wood (Mill Wood) ahead. Keep left alongside the wood, then go through two gates and over a little bridge to reach a road. Turn left and cross the river to reach **Michelham Priory**.

Continue along the lane to reach a road at a crossroads. Turn left to reach the Plough Inn, and go over a stile opposite, joining The Wealdway. With a hedge and fence to the right, make for the corner of Park Wood. Keep the wood on your left and walk on to reach a concrete crossing track. Go left, and right, by cottages, then cross the field ahead to reach a gate. Cross the next field to reach a footbridge, then go left beside a stream which joins the river. Just beyond, go past a small weir, then bear slightly right and through a gate. Keep close to the river until a bridge and stile is reached. Do not go over the big bridge: cross the smaller one, then go right, near the hedge, through a gate. The path soon turns left, avoiding a rough wet area. Keep this on the right, and bear round to reach a fence by Sessingham Farm. Keep the fence on your right go over a footbridge and under the pylon lines to reach a gate. Cross to the top right-hand corner of the next field, go through a gate and along a wooden fence to reach the path used on the outward journey. Turn right and follow the shore to the car park. From there, reverse the outward route, or follow the road back to the station.

POINTS OF INTEREST:

Arlington Church – The church has Saxon origins, fragments of medieval wall-paintings and a fine, recently made, font cover.

Michelham Priory – This Priory was founded by the Augustinians Order in 1229. The moat is one of the largest in England. The site, which also includes a Tudor barn, forge and water mill, is open to the public.

REFRESHMENTS:

The Berwick Inn, Berwick.
The Yew Tree, Arlington.
The Plough Inn, Upper Dicker.

Walks 62 & 63 THREE VILLAGES NEAR ARLINGTON   6¹/₂m (10¹/₂km) or 8¹/₂m (14 km)

Maps: OS Sheets Landranger 199; Pathfinder 1308.

A level field path walk, with a possible extension around the reservoir.

Start: At 510070, near Selmeston Church.

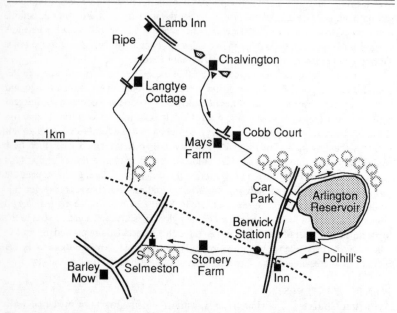

The walk starts about ¹/₂ mile (³/₄kms) south of the Barley Mow Inn on the A27.

Walk northwards from **Selmeston** Church and after about 400 yards turn left on to a footpath between houses. Go through a gate and bear half-right to cross three waymarked fields, heading towards a flint-walled barn. Now turn right through a gate, and cross the railway with great care. Go over a stile, then left to reach a footbridge. Go over and cross the field beyond to its top left corner. Maintain direction across the corners of the next two fields. Now in the large field ahead, keep round the left edges and go forward again, going under power lines to reach a stile on to a lane. Go through the gate by Langtye Cottage opposite to reach another gate. Go through and cross two

120

fields, going under more power lines. Now follow a path leading just to the left of **Ripe** Church. A short detour left here will bring you to the village and the Lamb Inn.

To continue, go along the right side of the churchyard to reach a gate. Go through and cross the next field. Go through a gap in the hedge ahead, beyond which the way is clear and straight, going over a little bridge and heading directly for **Chalvington** Church. At the church, turn right past a farm then go a little left and past a pond, on the left. Now go along the right sides of two fields, under the double power lines and left along the next field edge. After a further 100 yards, go on through a gap, and bear half-right across a field to reach a second gap. Continue half-right to emerge in a lane.

Maintain the same general direction, going left along the lane, and then turning right at a junction. About 500 yards further on, take the drive on the right, towards Mays Farm. Another 200 yards walking will bring you to the left of a fine house, Cobb Court. Go on over a jump to reach a little wooded area. Go through this to emerge on to a road.

For the longer walk, cross the road and go over a stile to reach a path near the edge of Arlington Reservoir. Turn left and follow waymarks round the shore to the dam. Walk along the top of the dam and follow the clear waymarks round Polhill's Farm to reach the Reservoir car park Now take the footpath to the left, going across fields to reach the Berwick Inn.

The shorter route continues along the road for $^1/_2$ mile ($^3/_4$kms) to reach Berwick railway station. Go over the level-crossing to reach the longer walk at the Berwick Inn. Opposite the inn, turn right along a footpath to reach a field corner and a large bridlegate. Keep ahead, leaving the railway line a little, half-left through a second gate and on, westerly, using a clear track for a full mile back to the church at Selmeston.

POINTS OF INTEREST:

Selmeston – The village has an interesting church, in the churchyard of which is a gravestone commemorating F. S. Mockford, originator of the 'Mayday' distress call.
Ripe – Do not miss, but gaze respectfully and mindful of good manners, at the highly decorated timber-framed cottage a few yards past The Lamb .
Chalvington – Another very pretty village and church.

REFRESHMENTS:
The Barley Mow, Selmeston.
The Lamb, Ripe.

Walk 64   **BRIGHTLING**   6$\frac{1}{2}$m (10$\frac{1}{2}$km)

Maps: OS Sheets Landranger 199; Pathfinder 1270.

Sussex High Weald, a folly and a 17th century manor, plus splendid views..

Start: At 684210, Brightling Church.

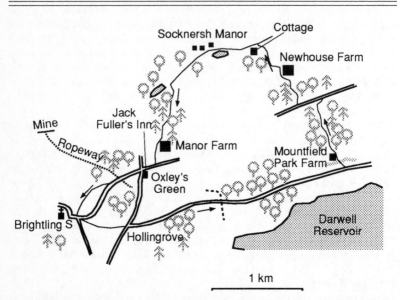

Leave **Brightling** village south-eastwards and at the road junction go ahead through a gateway between the roads. Follow the grassy, open path beyond to reach a wicket gate. Go through and along the left edge of the field beyond. As you maintain this, easterly, direction, Fuller's Tower can be seen to the right. The Tower should be visited: to do so, turn right along the obvious track. Retrace your steps and continue the walk by keeping along the left edge of another field. Join an access drive leading to cottages and a lane at Hollingrove. Go left, and right on the road towards **Mountfield** (as the signpost confirms!).

As you follow the quiet lane, there are fine views of the nearby Darwell Reservoir through the woods to the right. Leave the lane after about 1$\frac{3}{4}$ miles (3kms) going sharp left along the Mountfield Park Farm access road. Cross the Glottenham Stream on a small footbridge and then turn right, over a stile. Bear left across the corner of a field to reach another bridge and stile. Continue to a third stile, go over and climb up to reach a fourth into mixed woodland. Follow a path northwards through the wood to reach a lane. Turn left along the lane, passing cottages and Brightling Hall, and then turn right along the access lane to Newhouse Farm. Go between the buildings, with a fine converted oast-house to the right, and soon go left between shrubs to reach a stile. Go over and downhill to reach a bridge with a yellow waymark, following the path, as indicated, to reach a second bridge. Cross and go uphill, bearing half-left to pass to the right of a cottage. On reaching a corner, bear left between hedges and follow further waymarks to reach a lake and Socknersh Manor. Beside this fine house bear left to go over a stile. Go through a gate on to a drive and turn left along it. After passing another converted oast-house, to the left, turn right by a pond, and go over two stiles on the right Now go through woods to reach a road. Turn right to reach Oxley's Green and Jack Fuller's Inn at a junction. Take the road signed for Brightling, going under the conveyor from the gypsum mine. About 200 yards further on, go through a kissing-gate on the right and ascend along the left-hand hedge. Go between the power posts to join a hedge coming from the right, and continue to the top corner. There go over a stile, pausing for a final look back to the splendid view of Sussex before continuing along the path back the start of the walk.

POINTS OF INTEREST:

Brightling – 'Mad Jack Fuller' (1757 – 1834) lived in nearby Heathfield and caused many local oddities, including the Observatory, Temple, a Tower and a Needle, to be erected in order to provide employment for local men in those needy times. The pyramid in Brightling churchyard was supposed to contain Jack's body, top-hatted and sitting at a table with a glass of port in his hand. Sadly when it was opened recently it was empty – the mausoleum, that is not the glass!

Mountfield – Gypsum is extracted from the mines nearby. An aerial ropeway – which passes over the walk – connects the mines to the loading area from where the mineral is transported to be used in cement making, dental moulds and plasterboard manufacture.

REFRESHMENTS:
Jack Fuller's Inn, Oxley's Green.

Walk 65   **IDEN, THE ROTHER AND RYE** $6^1/_2$m ($10^1/_2$km)
Maps: OS Sheets Landranger 189; Pathfinder 1271.
Kent-Sussex borders, farmland, riverbank and the ancient Port of Rye.
Start: At 916238, between the church and the Bell Inn, Iden.

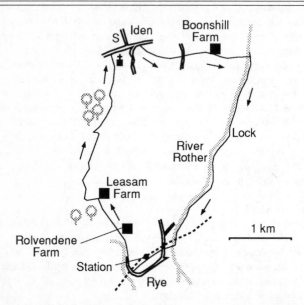

Walk past the Bell Inn on your left, to reach a road junction. Bear right, but then fork left on a road signposted Appledore. After about 120 yards, turn right along a footpath between houses, and then follow waymarks half-left across a field. Go across the next field and along the left edge of a third to reach a stile. Go over and to the left of a pond. Now keeping close to the left-hand hedge, go through a field to reach a road. Cross and follow the rough lane ahead to Boonshill Farm. Just beyond the farm, turn left on to a narrow path through scrub. Descend steeply into a gully, which can be slippery, and go down a grass cliff into the valley of the River Rother. Go past some cottages, walk along an access drive, go over a road and a bridge over the river, then turn right, along the riverbank. Now follow the river for 2 miles (3kms), with the town of **Rye** becoming ever-clearer ahead. After passing under a railway bridge, cross the river via the A259 to walk into the town.

To continue, make for the railway station. Now facing the station, turn left (south-westwards) and walk along to reach a bridge on the right. Cross the bridge (on the B2089) and shortly, on reaching the Queen Adelaide Inn, fork right alongside it. The road soon passes some houses and the River Tillingham on the left. About 400 yards further on, turn left over a stile and go forward across the pasture, aiming to pass to the left of some farm buildings which are ahead and to the right. Shortly beyond you should see a gate and stile: go through and climb up to the right to reach another stile in the top right corner. The path beyond leads across the top of Leasam Hill. Now, go across a drive, through a kissing-gate and into some trees. You emerge from the trees on to a farm road, with a converted oast-residence on the left. In front of this oast, turn right and descend on to a grassy path across the valley. The path climbs, becomes narrower and then reaches the A268 by going between a hedge and a fence. Turn left and go past Oak Tree Cottage. Now cross, with care, and go right through a gateway. Go along the right side of the field beyond to reach a corner. There go over a rough stile and make for a white-painted metal stile in a dip across the next field. Bear left around the field beyond the stile to another white stile. Go over and cross another field, making for the left of a bungalow. Two more stiles take you across a driveway about 50 yards left of the bungalow. The tower of Iden Church now offers a waymark ahead: pass to the left of some trees, go across a ditch and uphill into a recreation ground to reach the churchyard. From here it is a short step back to the start.

POINTS OF INTEREST:

Iden – A village on the very eastern edge of Sussex. There are traces of the Royal Military Canal which was, most oddly, dug (30 feet wide!) to repel a possible Napoleonic invasion in the early 1800's. It seems hardly likely to have deterred seasoned troops who had crossed such obstacles as the Danube, the Rhine and, by the time they landed here, the English Channel. The canal cost £200,000 – quite a sum in those days.

Rye – An ancient port of enormous historical interest, with many fine old buildings and literary connections – worth a lot of time to ramble and appreciate.

REFRESHMENTS:

The Bell Inn, Iden.
The Queen Adelaide Inn, Rye.
There are also numerous other possibilities in Rye.

Walks 66 & 67 PLUMPTON AND DITCHLING BEACON $6\frac{1}{2}$m ($10\frac{1}{2}$km) or 8m (13km)

Maps: OS Sheets Landranger 198; Pathfinder 1288.
A high point of the South Downs and several lowland villages.
Start: At 364132, the Half Moon public house, Plumpton.

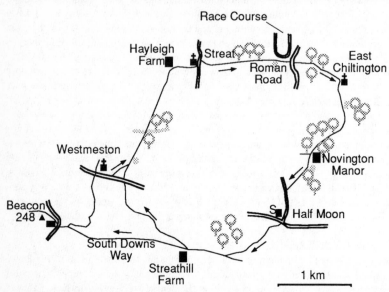

Opposite the Half Moon there is a 'bostal' – the Sussex word for steep track. Take this, follow up the face of the Downs to reach the South Downs Way at the top. The climb is soon well rewarded by the extensive views. Turn right and follow the Way westwards for about 400 yards, crossing a road from Streathill Farm.

For the shorter walk: fork right just past Streathill Farm to go through a fence-gate. Pass above a V-shaped plantation and then go downhill to reach several cross tracks. Go left towards some trees and continue down to reach the main B2116 road. Cross, with care, and go through iron gates into a garden. Now walk past barns to rejoin the longer walk.

For the longer walk: after crossing the road, continue ahead another $1\frac{1}{4}$ miles (2kms) to reach a car park and Ditchling Beacon, 813 feet (248m). From the car park and beacon, retrace the route for a few yards to find a double stile. Go over and bear left to descend diagonally, and steeply, passing some old quarries. Go through a gate and some trees to reach a road (the B2116) at **Westmeston.** Turn right along the road's verge and, about 100 yards after the church, turn left over a stile into a field. Go across the field to reach a second stile. Go over on to a track between a fence and a hedge, rejoining the shorter route.

The walks continue northwards to reach Hayleigh Farm. Here, turn right between tanks to reach a stile. Go over and cross the field beyond, then take a track leading to **Streat** Church. Beyond the church, turn left, and then right to go through the village. Now follow a wide track that leads almost due east and eventually reaches the race course, to the left, and a road. Cross the road and go through a gate opposite. The route now follows the course of a Roman road, to reach the wall of **East Chiltington** Church. Follow the wall round to the right and then bear left on a lane, with a lodge to the right. Stay on this lane, which leads south and south-west, passing woodland to the right. When the lane turns sharp right at Novington Manor, cross the stile ahead and go diagonally across a long paddock to reach a fence by some trees. Cross a field to the opposite corner and then go half-left to reach the road in **Plumpton** village. A left turn will now bring you back to the Half Moon.

POINTS OF INTEREST:

Westmeston – The church is dedicated to St Martin, the patron saint of publicans, even though there is no village pub. There are, though, many fine 17th century houses.
Streat – This beautiful village does not seem to have changed much over the centuries and is well worth the visit. It is certainly 'off the beaten track'.
East Chiltington – Do not miss the pub – it is used for parish meetings and elections, and was once thatched. The village church is 12th – 14th century.
Plumpton – This fine village is famous for its Agricultural College and National Hunt racecourse.

REFRESHMENTS:

The Half Moon, Plumpton (make a point of seeing the customers' mural).
The Jolly Sportsman, East Chiltington.
There is usually ice-cream at Ditchling Beacon.

Walk 68   SHORTGATE AND LAUGHTON   6¹/₂m (10¹/₂km)

Maps: OS Sheets Landranger 198 & 199; Pathfinder 1289.

A mixture of woodland and farm path walking.

Start: At 493150, the Bluebell Inn on the B2192 at Shortgate.

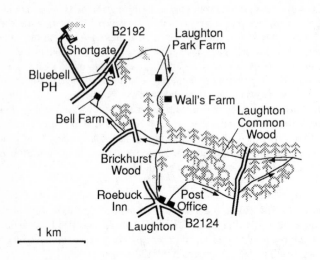

From the lay-by near the Bluebell Inn, head north-east for about 300 yards to reach a lane to Laughton. Just beyond this there is a concrete lane to the right of Manor Cottage. Walk along this, and when the concrete ends go through two gates and walk across three fields with hedges and ditches to the right. If there has been recent rain, a crossing ditch may require a small detour to the right, returning, via a gate, to the original easterly direction. Towards the end of the third field, turn right, go through an iron gate and at once go left through another gate to head towards a wireless mast. Cross a stile and a bridge in the next hedge and aim just left of the farm at Laughton Park. On arriving at the farm, go half-right along the access drive for about 350 yards, then go left along another drive, towards Wall's Farm. After about 120 yards this drive veers left by a bungalow: go straight ahead just inside a conifer plantation. Very soon the southerly direction is maintained by crossing a wire fence into the corner of a field: follow the hedge and ditch to the left, and cross the water by way of a wooden plank bridge. Now go straight across the next field, walking parallel to the hedge about 100 yards away to the left. Follow the path into Brickhurst Wood and, after a short distance, you will reach a broad crosstrack. Cross and continue ahead, still southerly, to reach a farm. Maintain the same general direction, passing a pond and reaching a lane leading to the Roebuck Inn at Laughton.

Turn left along the front of the inn, then go left again along the No Through Road by the Post Office. When the tarmac ends, go over the stile on the right and veer left across the narrow field beyond to reach a gate. Keep alongside the wood to the left – there are splendid views of Firle Beacon and the South Downs to the right – for $^1/_2$ mile to reach a lane. Turn left. After about 300 yards, just past a sawmill on the right, turn right over a stile on to a narrow path which soon widens and forks left, north-easterly through Laughton Common Wood when another, wide crossing track is reached, turn left, sharply back and head due west. Continue through the woodland to arrive back at the cross-track passed earlier. Do not retrace earlier steps: instead, keep ahead on the westerly route. The track becomes concreted and reaches a lane junction: take the lane opposite, signed for 'Lewes', and after about 100 yards turn right beside Little Common Wood, continuing to reach another junction – the path here is usually firm but can get muddy! Turn right at the junction, going past Bell Farm. After another 400 yards, turn left to regain the B2192 close to the Bluebell Inn.

The walk can end here but a worthwhile detour goes left for 400 yards. Now cross the road and follow the access road to **Bentley**. A $^1/_2$ mile walk along this reaches the very interesting Wildfowl and Motor Museum.

POINTS OF INTEREST:

Bentley – The wildfowl here include rare geese, ducks, swans and many other species, all viewable at close quarters. There is also a farmhouse, built post-war but in Georgian style, with fine furniture, paintings and wallpapers, a splendid formal garden and a very interesting collection of vintage vehicles, racing cars and military machines as well as a children's playground. There is even a woodland walk!

REFRESHMENTS:

The Bluebell Inn, Shortgate.
The Roebuck Inn, Laughton.
Refreshments are also available at Bentley.

Walk 69   MAGHAM DOWN AND COWBEECH   6½m (10½km)

Maps: OS Sheets Landranger 199; Pathfinder 1290.

Field and woodland paths north-east of Hailsham.

Start: At 608114, at Magham Down, just north of the Post Office on the A271.

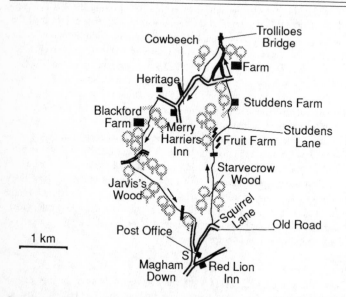

Start by walking along the minor road which forks left off the A271, Hailsham to Herstmonceux road. At the next fork, go right on 'The Old Road'. Just after a sharp right-hand bend, go ahead (NNE – *not* along Squirrel Lane which heads north-east) and cross a field. Go across the next field to reach Starvecrow Wood. Go through the wood, maintaining direction when you emerge, and keeping along the right side of three fields as you ascend towards buildings, to the left. Continue along a clear track to reach a road. Turn left, and at once right, between fruit farm buildings. You are now on Studdens Lane which will take you through an orchard, curving right and then left. Go into trees, over a footbridge and pass to the left of Studdens Farm. Continue northwards to reach a lane. Cross to another lane go straight ahead and follow it to a lane junction. Here, keep right to reach Trolliloes Bridge. Do not ascend the lane:

130

instead, go sharply left, uphill (heading south-west), keeping a small wood on the right. Go along the right edge of three fields to reach a crossing of paths. Keep straight on, along the edge of further fields to reach a lane at a bend. Go ahead, maintaining the south-westerly direction along the lane into Cowbeech, keeping left at a junction near the Merry Harriers Inn.

Turn right into Hammer Lane, leading to Warbleton, but after 550 yards, almost opposite 'Heritage', take the bridleway on the left and walk downhill. Go across a stream, into trees and under power lines. Maintain direction to go past a pond, to the right, turning right, then left, then going alongside a wood to the right. Finally you reach Cinderford Lane at a bend. Turn right along the lane for 500 yards, then look out for, and take, a footpath to the left and follow it into Jarvis's Wood. This pleasant track goes downhill at first, then crosses a stream and ascends. It leaves the wood and continues along the right edge of three fields to reach a road. Cross straight over and continue along the lane, passing a wood to the right. Follow the lane as it curves back to a junction with Old Road passed earlier on the walk. Turn right to regain the start at Magham Down.

POINTS OF INTEREST:
There are no specially interesting points on this walk, it is all good, though it can be muddy!

REFRESHMENTS:
The Red Lion, Magham Down.
The Merry Harriers, Cowbeech.

Walk 70   WOODINGDEAN AND THE JUGGS   7m (11km)

Maps: OS Sheets Landranger 198; Pathfinder 1307.

Remote downland, farms and fine views.

Start: At 356064, the northern edge of Woodingdean on the B2123.

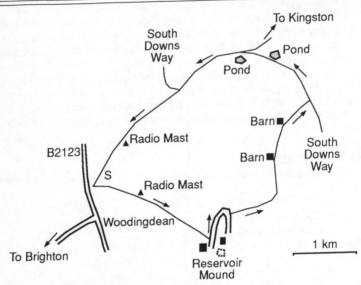

The start is at a rough parking area about 100 yards north of the factories on the outskirts of Woodingdean.

Leave the car park and take the track running eastward from the B2123, with the factories and houses on your right. After about $\frac{1}{2}$ mile (800 metres) go past a radio mast left, and a few hundred yards further on go over a crossing track. Go straight on, with houses now nearby on the right. Go slightly downhill, through a gate and along the right edge of a field, aiming for a mound ahead. This will soon appear as a grassy reservoir: go through a gate, under the power lines and then curve left across a field to join a concrete road at another gate. Go through the gate and descend sharply to reach the road, which soon doubles back to the right. Do not follow it: instead, keep left, go through another gate and, when the track beyond curves left, go through yet another gate and up the hill ahead. After about $\frac{1}{2}$ mile (800 metres), as the path levels, go through a gate by a cattle trough. Now turn left, heading towards a barn. Keep to the right of this and go over the open downland ahead to reach a second barn. Again keep this on the left. The track ahead becomes more distinct as a ridge overlooking the **Ouse Valley** is approached. As the firm concrete turns right, keep ahead to reach a gate. Go through, turn left and follow the wire fence on the left, and enjoying the views above Iford, Kingston and Lewes. You are now on part of the **South Downs Way**. (There are refreshments at Kingston but reaching them means a very steep descent and ascent, plus two extra miles.)

The Way is clear: follow it for about a mile ($1\frac{1}{2}$ kms). On reaching a pond, to the right, bear left between posts. Soon a second pond is seen, to the left, where a track comes up from Kingston. At this point you are on the **Juggs Road**: after another $\frac{3}{4}$ mile ($1\frac{1}{4}$ kms) the South Downs Way swings right to follow the fence to the right, but the route keeps to the higher path, going through a wide, grassy and scrubby area, and heading for a radio mast. In due course the path becomes rough and stony: stay on it to return to the starting point.

POINTS OF INTEREST:

Ouse Valley – The River Ouse was once navigable for seagoing ships to sail as far inland as Lewes.

The South Downs Way – This National Trail was officially opened in July 1972. It has two starts in Eastbourne and ends near Winchester. Much of it follows an ancient trackway used by Stone Age man.

Juggs Road – The road ran from Brighton to Lewes and is said to have been used by smugglers. It was certainly used by Brighton fishermen's wives to sell their catches in Lewes. The name derives from the men who were nicknamed Juggs.

REFRESHMENTS:

None en route but available in nearby Woodingdean.

Walk 71 ALCISTON, WEST FIRLE AND THE BEACON 7m (11km)
Maps: OS Sheets Landranger 199; Pathfinder 1308.
An old Coach Road and good ridge walk.
Start: At 505055, Alciston.

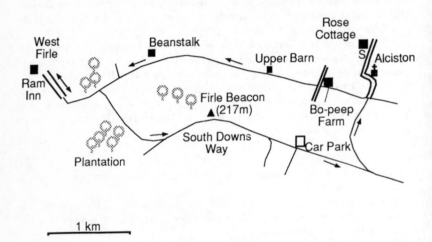

West Firle • Ram Inn • Beanstalk • Upper Barn • Rose Cottage • Alciston • Firle Beacon ▲(217m) • Bo-peep Farm • South Downs Way • Car Park • Plantation

1 km

Please park carefully in the village of **Alciston**, and then walk south-westward towards The Downs. The village's splendid tithe barn is on the left. Follow the lane left and right until a clear track coming from the left is reached. Turn right on to the track and continue north-westerly, going alongside two fields, to reach the barns and house of Bo-peep. Cross the metalled road and walk straight ahead along the old coach road, very muddy at times, going past cottages (Upper Barn and Beanstalk). When a pair of old cottages appears ahead, fork left and go around the boundary of Firle Place. After about 500 yards, the track turns right – often muddily! – into Place Farm. Follow the clear way through the farm and into the village of **West Firle**, where the Ram Inn is a good resting place.

Retrace your steps to the church and Place Farm, and follow the old track along which you came as it turns left back towards Bo-peep. Now, however, after about 400 yards a footpath to the right is reached. Take this, going, to the left of a hedge and, soon after, going alongside Firle Plantation, on your right, and very steeply uphill. Nearing the top the pitch eases a little as the path turns gently left, and in due course the summit and the South Downs Way are reached. Turn left along the Way, following it for the next 2 miles (3kms), passing the trig. point at Firle Beacon (217 metres). On this section of the route you can look down on the Coach Road used earlier, as well as on the traffic on the A27 trunk road which has replaced it. Running parallel to both is the railway line from Eastbourne to Lewes.

Continue along the long distance footpath, with fenced farmland to the right, going through gates by the top of Bo-peep Bostal and a car park. Now go straight uphill and, just over the brow of the hill, bear left across open downland to reach a stile in the fence. Go over and follow the path beyond downhill, going slightly left and then steeply down, to reach another stile. Go over and walk towards Alciston tithe barn and village, going through a woody area to reach the footpath intersection where the walk began.

POINTS OF INTEREST:

Alciston – Look out for the church on its little hill, the medieval dovecote and the great tithe barn (170 feet long) which was a storage place for the monks of Battle Abbey.

West Firle – Firle Place, home of the Gage Family, is open to the public during the summer and contains many fine pictures and furniture. It has associations with early USA history and with greengages!

There are two sundials on the village church wall, but they are on the north wall where the sun never casts a shadow. Can you solve this mystery?

The village itself is particularly attractive, not only for the alabaster figures and brasses in the church, but the cast-iron house numbers and the house hung with mathematical tiles made to look like bricks.

REFRESHMENTS:

The Rose Cottage, Alciston.
The Ram Inn, West Firle.

Walk 72 Eastbourne, Jevington and the Wealdway 7m (11km)

Maps: OS Sheets Landranger 199; Pathfinder 1324.

Downland tops, lovely village and the start of a long distance footpath.

Start: At 588991, near the YHA building on the A259, 1 mile west of Eastbourne.

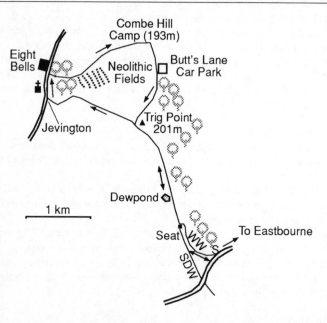

Take the track just below the Youth Hostel, climbing up through trees and bushes to reach a golf course. You are now on the **Wealdway** and will soon enjoy increasingly extensive views, to the right, across Eastbourne to Pevensey, Hastings and Fairlight. Go behind a stone-backed seat by a putting green, having now joined the **South Downs Way**, an official National Trail, and continue northwards along a clear track (there are several, but they all run parallel) through the gorse. Keep on the high contour, going past a large dewpond and continuing with open downland to the right and field fences to the left. Follow the curving fence as it bends left to reach the meeting of several tracks by a trig. point (201 metres). Go left, downhill, following a signpost for Jevington. The track is deeply cut into the chalk, brightly white in dry weather but very slippery in the wet. You have now left the Wealdway, but are still on the South Downs Way which descends towards a stile. Go over and cross to a fence in the left corner of a field. There, take the path through a small wooded area to emerge in a green pasture with steep sides and head for a stile by cottages on the edge of **Jevington** village. Take the lane ahead to reach the main village road near the tearooms and a restaurant. Turn right and follow the road with care to reach a pavement which appears to the left. Now follow the pavement to reach the Eight Bells, a most suitable resting place.

The walk now rejoins the Wealdway by taking the track opposite the Eight Bells. This goes steeply up, with hedges to the right, climbing the flank of **Combe Hill,** to the left. When the built up area of Eastbourne appears ahead and below, turn right along the ridge, making for a gate and the car park at Butt's Brow about $^1/_2$ mile ($^3/_4$kms) further south. Keep right of the car park, still walking southerly, and follow the clear track to reach the trig. point and cross tracks passed earlier on the walk. Now retrace your steps, with the Channel to the left and ahead, for a splendid mile back to the golf course, then fork left through the rough and bushes to the start.

POINTS OF INTEREST:
The Wealdway – This excellent long distance footpath begins at Eastbourne and runs 80 miles to Gravesend.
The South Downs Way – This National Trail was officially opened in July 1972. It has two starts in Eastbourne and ends near Winchester. Much of it follows an ancient trackway used by Stone Age man.
Jevington – The village has a collection of fine flint-walled buildings, a church dedicated to St Andrew (look for a bronze model of a fully-rigged frigate in the churchyard, a memorial to a Liverpool Shipowner) and other, refreshing attractions.
Combe Hill – In the time of Abraham (the Neolithic era) there were farmers here, living in an enclosure on the hill top (at 193 metres) with their flocks and farming the lower slopes. Numerous tumuli in the area between the Camp and Butt's Brow would suggest important people were buried here, too.

REFRESHMENTS:
The Eight Bells, Jevington.
As mentioned in the text, there are also tearooms and a restaurant in the village.

Walk 73   **BUXTED AND THE MAYPOLE**   7m (11km)

Maps: OS Sheets Landranger 198 and 199; Pathfinder 1269.

Easy walking on farmland paths and a deer park.

Start: At 497233, Buxted Railway Station.

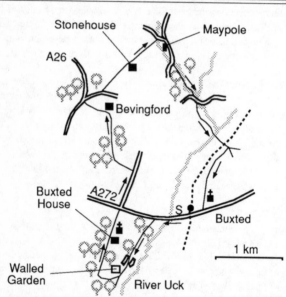

Leave the railway station and turn right (westward) on the A272. Cross the River Uck and after about 200 yards, just past the lodge, turn left through a wooden gate into **Buxted Park**. Keep left and walk parallel with the river and railway. The path runs between two lakes, then alongside a walled garden to the right: at the garden corner turn right, looking for the Wealdway's reassuring WW signs. After about 350 yards, turn right again, staying on the Wealdway to go over a stile. Go past the church, to the right, and walk on to reach the A272 again.

Turn right, cross the road with care, and then immediately go left, following the signposted lane for High Hurstwood. Walk along the lane for about 600 yards, then go over a stile on the left and walk across a field to reach a gate. Go through and bear right, over some railings, to descend steeply and half-right to reach a footbridge. Cross and maintain direction as you go gently uphill towards some buildings. On reaching 'Bevingford', keep left and walk to a main road (A26). Turn right, and immediately right again into Rocks Lane. As the lane bends right, go left into the drive for 'Stonehouse'. Walk forward for $^1/_2$ mile ($^3/_4$kms), ignoring a left fork, then go through wrought iron gates. Beyond, walk between hedges, continuing for another $^1/_2$ mile ($^3/_4$kms), and passing 'Parkhurst' to reach a lane.

Turn right, then right again to walk past the Maypole Inn. **Maypole Farm** is on the right here. Continue along the lane, then turn left into the White Coppice drive. Go right over two stiles, and follow the stream on your right to reach a footbridge. Cross and go left through a gate – the stream is now on your left. Walk past an unusual sandstone outcrop, beyond which the path narrows and goes between hedges to reach a lane. Go left, over the stream, then right over a stile. Keep left of the field beyond, following the stream also on the left, and as it bends further left, go straight on, cross a footbridge and ascend to another, this time over railway lines. Cross the bridge and turn right at once to walk parallel to the line. Now take the drive forking left at St Margaret's Cottage and follow it to reach a lane. Turn right along the lane, following it back into Buxted and the start of the walk.

POINTS OF INTEREST:
Buxted Park – Buxted is still a fine wooded deer park in spite of the ravages of the 1987 gale. Look out for the impressive main entrance to Buxted House and the ha-ha, a sunken wall in a ditch to keep cattle out of the garden!
Maypole Farm – This is a fifteenth century timber-framed house in fine condition.

REFRESHMENTS:
The Maypole Inn, High Hurstwood.
A variety of refreshments may be found in Buxted.

Walk 74   FLETCHING AND THE FOREST FRINGES   7m (11km)

Maps: OS Sheets Landranger 198; Pathfinder 1269.

Lanes and field paths on the southern fringes of Ashdown Forest.
Start: At 428235, in Fletching village.

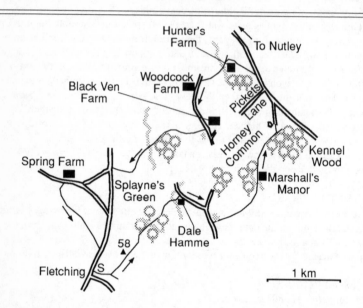

Begin by walking down **Fletching** village street to reach the Griffin Inn, on the right. Now go left on a path into the churchyard. At the far end, go through a gate and bear half-left across the field beyond to reach a stile in the far corner. Go over and, following the yellow arrows, make for the next stile. Go over on to an enclosed path, following it across the next field and down to a stream with a plank bridge. Yellow markers beyond the bridge will reassure you about the way ahead, pointing the way across fields to a half-timbered house, Dale Hamme, in a lane. Turn right here and walk to a junction. There, bear right for about 200 yards and then go left through a gate. Walk past a pond, to the right and cross the brow of a hill. Now make for the end of the row of trees, to the left, to reach a stile. Go over and continue to follow the waymarks – the general direction is now northerly – to pass to the left of the sandstone Marshall's Manor. Keep on the Manor's access drive, going over a crossing track.

Bear left, between houses, to defer reaching the busy A22, although this is unavoidable after another 500 yards when the lane joins the main road. Turn left – great care is required here – and continue past Picketts Lane, left, and another lane, right. After a further 100 yards, just past two houses, go half-left and diagonally across a field. Now go along the left edge of two small fields behind Hunter's Farm. On reaching the farm's track, turn left and go gently uphill to reach a lane by Woodcock's Farm. Turn left along the lane to reach Black Ven Farm. Just past the buildings go through a gate on the right, with pond to the left. The route is now westerly, across fields and over stiles for $\frac{1}{2}$ mile ($\frac{3}{4}$kms), passing a conifer wood, a paddock and a cottage to join a driveway. Follow this down to a road, north of Splayne's Green. Turn left, then immediately right along another quiet lane to reach a junction. Keep ahead, and just after passing Spring Farm, to the right, take the footpath on the left. The path leads across several fields, south-easterly, going through gates and gaps and returning to Fletching close to the Rose and Crown Inn. From there it is a short step back to the start.

POINTS OF INTEREST:

Fletching – The church contains the remains of at least three notables: Peter Dynot was one of Jack Cade's fellow-rebels. The rebels were so dissatisfied with the current political situation they marched on London (1450), seized the Tower and generally upset the status quo. The author of 'The Decline and Fall of the Roman Empire', Edward Gibbon is also buried here as is Richard Leche, a local landowner. The inscription on Leche's monument is well worth reading.

REFRESHMENTS:
The Griffin Inn, Fletching.
The Rose & Crown, Fletching.

Walk 75   **WITHYHAM**   7m (11km)

Maps: OS Sheets Landranger 188; Pathfinder 1248
Forest tracks and field paths, and the Buckhurst Estate.
Start: At 495326, Church Hill car park.

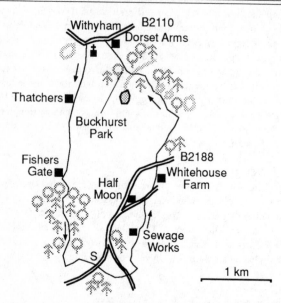

The car park is on the B2188, north-west of Crowborough.

From the car park cross the road and take the bridleway going left and downhill. Go over another clear track to reach a track junction. Go left and down to a road. Turn right, go over a bridge and then left through a gate leading to Friar's Gate Farm. Immediately go left on to an enclosed path. Go over a footbridge and up steps into a field. Follow the field edge to the right as it bends round, then go over stiles to reach a farm drive. Just before the farmyard, go into the field on the right and keeping the hedge on your right, walk down to reach a concrete lane to the right of the sewage works. Turn right and follow the lane to a road. To reach the Half Moon Inn, go left along the road. The walk continues by crossing the road and keeping ahead (that is, bearing slightly right) for 300 yards to pass Whitehouse Farm. Continue to reach the B2188.

142

Cross the road and follow the lane opposite as it ascends and curves right. Look for a stile to the left, up the bank about 300 yards from the road, and go over it into a field. Go up the field, keeping close to the hedges on the right. Keep right of the highest point of the field, and make for the left corner of Coppice Wood. On reaching the wood, keep it on your right, and go downhill towards the bottom right corner. Go through a gate on the right, just before the corner, to reach a lane and a curving track on the left. This is Buckhurst Park. At the lake keep left and follow the path to **Withyham** and the Dorset Arms.

Follow the village road (the B2110) round to reach the churchyard gate, on the left. Go through and walk up to the West Door to explore the church. On leaving, go left (south-west) to reach a private road leading to Buckhurst Farm and Fisher's Gate. This is a public footpath. Follow the road for a mile (1^1/$_2$kms), with splendid views. Go across cattle grids at Fisher's Gate, then go through a gate on the left into woodland. Keep ahead past a house (to the right,) with fine gates, but soon fork left. Now walk south for another mile. Just after the turn to Pimp Barn, curve right and go round a pond to reach a cross track. Go straight across and maintain direction to reach a gate. Go through into a plantation. Keep along the right-hand edge, then go left around the bottom to reach a path. Now follow the path back to the starting point.

POINTS OF INTEREST:

Withyham – Withyham Church has 14th-century foundations, but was rebuilt in 1662 after being struck by lightning. The Dorset Arms is a fine 16th-century inn. A detour of about 400 yards to the east of the inn will bring you to 'Duckings', a mid-Tudor house of special architectural interest.

REFRESHMENTS:

The Half Moon, just off the route.
The Dorset Arms, Withyham.

Walk 76 ISFIELD AND BARCOMBE MILLS 7m (11km)

Maps: OS Sheets Landranger 198; Pathfinder 1289.

Easy walk through a fine wood and along the banks of the upper Ouse.

Start: At 452172, in Isfield.

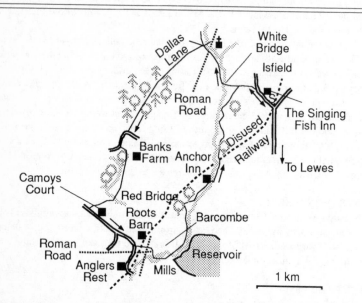

Pass the quaintly named Singing Fish Inn, **Isfield,** on your right, and shortly after the telephone exchange, also on the right, turn left along the tarmac lane just to the left of the cricket field. The lane soon becomes a track: keep ahead, passing an attractive pond and buildings, left, to reach White Bridge. Cross the bridge and turn right along the riverbank. The path is sometimes indistinct and leaves the bank for a few yards to return again later. Further on, with the spire of Isfield Church across the river, and shortly after a 'Private Fishing' sign, go through an iron gate in a field corner and turn left along the clear track beyond. This is Dallas Lane. Follow the track through conifers and deciduous trees, passing a cross-track with a seat and four concrete blocks, and ignoring all paths, left and right, to reach a gate between cottages and with a built-in stile. Go through, leaving the wood, and go forward to reach a tarmac road.

Go ahead, following the road downhill for 400 yards to where it turns right. Here, turn left along the access road to Banks Farm. After a few yards turn right at a gate and stile, into a field. Cross the field corner towards a large tree in the hedge opposite and walk down to reach another gate. Go through, but do not go uphill: instead, go ahead, along the middle of the park-like meadows with a stream to the right and a fence up to the left. When the river and fence meet by a gate and stile, go over and forward for 30 yards, then turn right across a footbridge over a pretty weir and sluice. This is Red Bridge. Go across the left corner of the field ahead to reach a gate and stile. Go over and uphill, following yellow waymarks over further stiles to reach a road at Camoys Court. This road is busy so take care as you turn left and follow it. Ignore a lane signposted to Hamsey and go past Crink House and Roots Barn. Now, as the road bends right, go ahead at a finger post. Go across and down a field past some cottages, to the left, to reach a stile. Cross and go over a disused railway line with the aid of two flights of steps to emerge in a lane. Turn left, and after 100 yards turn right between buildings and go down to **Barcombe Mills**.

Go over two substantial bridges and then go left through a squeeze stile, with the River Ouse to the left. Keep along the riverbank, then go left over a bridge with two squeeze stiles. Turn right, with the river now on the right – and Barcombe Reservoir up the bank beyond it – and follow yellow waymarks as you cross two more bridges. Shortly before a weather-boarded cottage, go left and then right, passing behind the cottage and one of many local 1939–45 War pillboxes. Now continue along the path to reach the Anchor Inn. There cross another bridge, to the right and then turn left along the riverbank. Go under a low disused railway bridge and across meadows, making for a rusty red-roofed barn, to reach another gate and stile. Go over on to the lane used during the early part of the walk. Turn right and go past a little pond, to the right, and out to a road. Turn right to reach the starting point.

POINTS OF INTEREST:
Isfield – While you are in the village, be sure to take time to admire the restored Southern Railway station, the large mill and the pound.
Barcombe Mills – There is much to enjoy at this delightful spot – the pools and weirs, the toll bridge charges from 1939, and the trout, which can often be seen.

REFRESHMENTS:
The Singing Fish Inn, Isfield.
The Anglers Rest , Barcombe Mills.
The Anchor Inn , on the route.

Walk 77 **NEWHAVEN** 7m (11km)

Maps: OS Sheets Landranger 198; Pathfinder 1308.

A walk of contrasting interests: ships, seabirds, lonely downland and a riverbank.

Start: At 447015, the swing bridge at Newhaven.

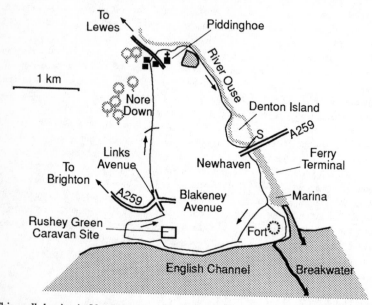

This walk begins in **Newhaven,** on the A259 just before the swing bridge over the River Ouse.

Turn so as to have the fascinating harbour on your left hand. Now walk past a fishing fleet, ships, chandlers, a ferry and a new Marina. Continue along Fort Road, then turn right on a track going uphill to the right of the Fort. (A detour to The Hope Inn, and a bracing walk along the breakwater are also recommended. This, and the return, will add 1$\frac{1}{2}$ miles to the walk length.) Go through a 'Keep Clear' barrier and, after 50 yards, fork left through bushes to reach the cliff edge – with the usual caution! Turn right to enjoy channel views, wheeling seabirds, views of Brighton and, perhaps, Selsey and the Isle of Wight ahead, and an excellent mile of walking on a clear path.

146

When the first bungalows are about 100 yards ahead, turn right and go right again soon to the Rushey Green Caravan Park. Turn left into Blakeney Avenue, cross the A259, very carefully, and go into Links Avenue opposite. The route is now northwards, passing through a gate, then going between paddocks and crossing downland, with gorse and other bushes and, probably, skylarks. Walk for $\frac{1}{2}$ mile before veering a little right and descending along a ridge, with Piddinghoe Church spire ahead and the meandering River Ouse off to the right. Away to the right and ahead are Firle Beacon and Mount Caburn. Continue the descent of Nore Down to find a track joining from the left. This leads between farm outbuildings and on to the Lewes – Newhaven road. This road is often busy, so take care as you cross to the little path opposite. Follow the path into **Piddinghoe**. Turn right along the main village street, then go left along the lane to the church. Skirt to the left of the church to join the raised river bank, which swings east at first, then southwards. Follow the river bank into Newhaven. As the bank ends, take the narrow path through to a road. This turns left towards the swing bridge where the walk began.

POINTS OF INTEREST:

Newhaven – When Seaford's harbour silted up and a great storm diverted the River Ouse in medieval times the little village of Meeching developed into a 'new haven' and expanded to become an important ship building centre. Now it is mainly a Ferry Terminal, though there are still some fishing boats and a little commercial seagoing traffic. Be sure to look for the dredgers, cabin cruisers, the pilot launch and the lifeboat as well as ships from abroad flying their national flag. They also fly the British 'red duster' amidships as a mark of respect. Newhaven was the main assembly-point for the ill-fated 1942 Dieppe raid and was also used as an embarkation point for troops involved in the D-Day landings. The fort passed on the walk was built in the 1860's to resist a possible French invasion and its recent restoration makes it an interesting site to visit.

Piddinghoe – The village offers a colourful picture when its 'pond' is full of little yachts and gliding swans. Note also the church of St John with its round Norman tower and its gilded dolphin (or is it a sea trout?). There is also a fine modern stained-glass window. In the garden of Kiln Cottage is a bottle-shaped brick kiln, probably the only one of its kind in England. It was last used in 1912, but was restored in 1980.

REFRESHMENTS:

The Hope Inn, Newhaven.
The Royal Oak, Piddinghoe.

Walk 78   SOUTH OF SEDLESCOMBE   7m (11km)

Maps: OS Sheets Landranger 199; Pathfinders 1290 and 1291.
Woods, fields and valleys five miles north of Hastings.
Start: At 781180, in Sedlescombe, on the A229.

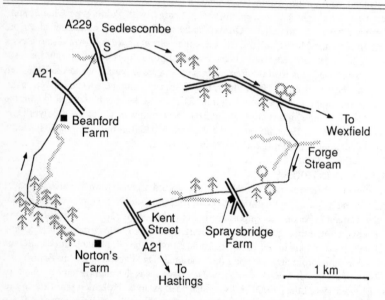

Starting in **Sedlescombe,** walk south past the Coach and Horses Inn and turn left into the recreation ground. Follow the River Brede for 400 yards, then cross a stile. Follow the bank again, then go diagonally across a narrow field. When level with a farm on the right, go right, cross a bridge and go over a stile into a field. Turn left and follow the hedge to a copse. Go through the copse and over a stile into the field ahead. Now make for the group of beech trees. Go over another stile and into a copse. Go through and continue to reach some pine trees and, beyond, a kissing-gate. Go across a track and through another small area of woodland to reach a road. Turn left.

When the main power lines cross the road, about 200 yards ahead, look for a concrete footpath sign on the right. Take this, descending to the corner of a field. Go over a stile and continue to reach a plank bridge over Forge Stream. Cross and turn right, heading for a bush to the right of a wooden pole. Cross a second plank bridge

148

and follow the stream bank for 400 yards. Now veer right along the hedge which comes down from the right, and after about 100 yards go right again to the edge of a spinney. Turn right, then go over a stile into pasture. Go a little left to reach another plank bridge by some trees. Cross into the next field and go along the right-hand edge. Go over a little bridge and a stile to reach a road, near Spraysbridge Farm. Turn right for 30 yards, then go left (westward) through a gate into a field. Continue westward, at first keeping bushes, then a stream to the left as you go through fields. Go over a bridge, under a power line and over another bridge. Continue following the bushes and stream on the right to reach a sign. Turn left to reach the busy A21. With due care, turn left for 100 yards, then cross and turn right up the access track to Norton's Farm.

Go through the farm, pass a pond and head westward, following the hedges to the end of a field where there is a gateway. In the next field maintain direction to reach the edge of Battle Great Wood. Go through another gate into the conifer wood. At the first junction of paths, turn left, and descend. Go left again at the next junction and walk down to a cross-tracks. Turn right, but after about 220 yards, where the path turns sharply left take the narrow path on the right. Follow this to a stile into a large field. Follow the field path to Beanford Farm. Go through and walk down the access drive to reach the A21 again. Cross with the utmost caution and go through the gate opposite. Go left, then right to reach a gap in the hedge which leads to a plank bridge over a stream. Cross, go left along a fence-line, over another bridge and, very soon, go left over a third bridge. Maintain direction to reach a larger bridge, and some silver birch trees and the walk's start back in Sedlescombe.

POINTS OF INTEREST:

Sedlescombe – With its long and narrow green the village is a place to wander and admire. There are weather-boarded and tile-hung Georgian houses, a lead covered pump and a smart village sign. It was a centre of Sussex iron-producing and, later, gun-powder making. Pestalozzi Children's Village, founded by Johann Henrich Pestalozzi (1746 – 1827) a Swiss educational theorist, can be visited by prior arrangement (Tel: 0424 870444).

REFRESHMENTS:

The Coach and Horses, Sedlescombe.
There are also other possibilities in Sedlescombe.

Walk 79   HARTFIELD   7m (11km)

Maps: OS Sheets Landranger 188; Pathfinder 1248.
A fine walk passing many 'Pooh' landmarks.
Start: At 478357 in Hartfield.

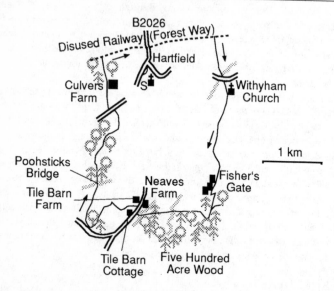

After walking along the lane between the Hay and Waggon and the Anchor in
Hartfield, turn left through the arch and go alongside the churchyard. Go past the
school, then go through a kissing-gate and on to a road junction. Go ahead (on the
B2026) and, just before a bridge, turn right and go through a gate. Walk past a house,
to the right, which was once the railway station and after a further 50 yards turn right
on to Forest Way, once the railway line, and follow it for $^3/_4$ mile. On arriving at the
second crossing path, go right (south) over a stile on to the Wealdway. Follow the
Way, and its yellow markers, southwards as it crosses the B2110 and passes to the
right of the church in **Withyham**. Then 50 yards past the cottages of Fisher's Gate,
turn left by the gate and go between fences and then right into woodland 50 yards
further on. At a lane junction, take the lane ahead and after 100 yards fork right by a
cottage. After another 120 yards, fork right again on to a forestry track. You are now

walking westward, still on the Wealdway: go past Kovacs Lodge, staying on the woodland path just inside Five Hundred Acre Wood ('Hundred Aker' according to Christopher Robin). Do not go further into the woods (!) but, soon after crossing a small footbridge, go right and uphill to the wood edge. There, go right again to reach a road opposite Tile Barn Cottage. Turn right along the road for 75 yards, then go left towards to Tile Barn Farm – 'Wol's' House was in a nearby tree. Turn left after the first barn, go on for 150 yards, then go through the furthest left of three gates. Now go along the hedge to enter a field. Cross this, maintaining direction to enter Posingford Wood. When confronted by three alternative paths, take the middle one, soon crossing a hurdle into a paddock. Go through the gate in the far corner then go left along the field edge to a reach second hurdle. Now turn right on a track leading to a tarmac lane.

Go straight along the lane for 50 yards, then turn right through a gate and descend to Poohsticks Bridge. Cross and continue. A lane comes in from the left and, a short distance further on, another comes in from the right: keep straight on, then, after another 100 yards, turn right through a gate into a field. Keep along the left edge of the field, then turn right at the end and cross a stile into the corner of a wood. Off to the right at this point is Cotchford Farm, where A. A. Milne once lived. Go diagonally across the field ahead to reach a stile to the left of a brick house. Go over and across a tarmac path. Turn right through a gate and go along a path with woods to the left until, about 150 yards further, you can turn right by a fence in front of a house. Cross a stile, go left along a fence and over another stile to find a gate at a field corner. Go through and down to reach the B2110 close to the Gallipot Inn, which is to the left, about 250 yards away. Now either turn right along B2110 back to Hartfield, or continue northwards, following a bridleway to Culvers Farm. Go through the wood beyond to rejoin the Forest Way on the disused railway. Turn right, to return to the old station, and then reverse the outward route back to the start in Hartfield.

POINTS OF INTEREST:

Hartfield – Has an attractive 15th-century church with an unusual lych gate adjacent to a cottage, as well as the 'Pooh Corner' shop full of A. A. Milne memorabilia.
Withyham – Withyham Church has 14th-century foundations, but was rebuilt in 1662 after being struck by lightning. The Dorset Arms is a fine 16th-century inn. A detour of about 400 yards to the east of the inn will bring you to 'Duckings', a mid-Tudor house of special architectural interest.

REFRESHMENTS:
The Hay and Waggon, Hartfield.
The Anchor Inn, Hartfield.

Walk 80 BRIGHTON MARINA AND ROTTINGDEAN   7m (11km)

Maps: OS Sheets Landranger 198; Pathfinder 1307.

A classic walk: cliff and undercliff plus historical associations.

Start: At 333033, Kemp Town, near Brighton Marina.

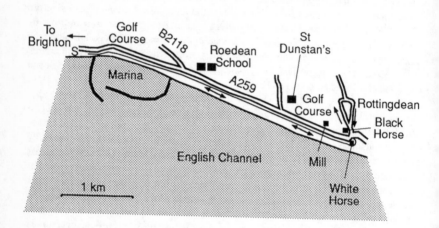

Directions for this walk are very simple to follow. The points of interest are manifest and manifold, and a very wide variety of refreshments are available at the halfway point.

Begin at the eastern end of Brighton's seafront near the recently constructed Marina and walk towards Newhaven. You will need to decide whether to walk out under the cliffs and back on the cliff tops or vice versa. However, it is prudent to do the undercliff walking at low tide or when it is ebbing, although there are steps to escape up to safety at Ovingdean, and to have the usually breeze clifftop walk when the tide is flowing or high. Assuming the tide is low, walk the 3 miles along the undercliff promenade, heading eastwards and noting the interesting rock formations, the chalk, made of billions of tiny organisms, the blackish flint and the shallow soil. Rock pools abound, awaiting inspection and wonder. The 'prom' was built by Welsh miners during an earlier economic recession and there are remnants of the Volks Railway which once ran along the beach but was gradually washed away by damaging tides and storms. Eventually you will arrive at steps on the left that lead up to the White Horse at Rottingdean. Cross the busy A259 and walk along the High Street. Here, the Black Horse is a Tudor building, while the tea-shop called 'Old Cottage' is more than 300 years old. The former village square is on the left with a school founded in 1855 and several charming old houses. The walk soon reach The Dene where the wife-to-be of Stanley Baldwin lived: Kipling resided in The Elms before buying Batemans in Burwash. Other residents of Rottingdean included the Pre-Raphaelite painter Edward Burne-Jones and the designer William Morris. Lutyens, the architect, designed alterations to the old Grange which is now a good Museum and Art Gallery where the visitor can see Kipling memorabilia and a toy collection.

In pre-electricity days a German bank clerk named Reuter also lived here. He began a pigeon post to bring news from overseas thus starting the Reuter's News Agency. Towards the end of the century the painter William Nicholson (who lived in the Grange) sketched the Black Smock Mill nearby, and his sketch was later adopted by the publishers Heinemanns as their trademark.

The church, dedicated to St Margaret, has fine stained glass windows (by Burne-Jones). The Baldwins were married here. Much earlier it had been burnt by raiding Frenchmen (in 1377, though marks of the burning can still be seen on parts of the building). In the 1940's, the church was almost bought and taken to the USA, but an exact replica was made instead. In the churchyard can be seen the graves of, among some of others mentioned above, G. H. Elliott of old music hall fame and the novelist Angela Thirkell. Returning to the A259 the walk heads westward, along the clifftops. Try to ignore the noise and fumes of the busy road and to concentrate on the Channel views. Brighton, Hove and Selsey are ahead, Newhaven and Seaford behind and to the east. Inland is the mill, St Dunstan's home for the blind, with its many guide-rails, and the imposing Girls School at Roedean. Finally you can view the many fine vessels in the Marina before returning to the start of the walk.

POINTS OF INTEREST:
As described within the walk description above.

REFRESHMENTS:
Numerous(!) including some mentioned in the walk description above.

Walk 81   **ASHURST WOOD**   7m (11km)

Maps: OS Sheets Landranger 188; Pathfinder 1248.
A fine Wealden walk.
Start: At 419366, the church at Ashurst Wood.

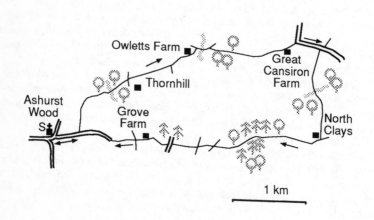

From the church, walk east, ignoring Maypole Road, to the left, to go into the 'No Through Road'. After 400 yards, turn left into School Lane, going past the school and continuing northwards, along what the OS map marks as 'Dirty Lane'!. Ignore two alternatives, leading left, following the lane as it turns eastward into woodland. Beyond, it crosses a little stream and then ascends. Go directly over at a cross-drive and descend along the left edge of fields to pass to the right (south) of Owlett's Farm. Cross a stile and footbridge to join a fenced path leading right and uphill. After a further 200 yards turn left over two more stiles, then go right, following the power lines. Now keep a wood (Holden Wood) on your right, go over another stile and cross two fields, staying close to the power lines. Go down, then up and a little left along a bridleway that goes between the buildings of Great Cansiron Farm. Follow the farm's access drive out to a lane and turn right.

Follow the lane for 400 yards to reach a concrete footpath marker by a hedge-gap to the left. Follow this, heading southward across a field. Go through a hedge-gap and maintain direction to reach the left corner of a wood. There, cross a little bridge and ascend, with the wood on your right. At the end of the wood, bear a little left, going under more power lines, then bear right along the edge of a field to reach a gateway in the corner. Continue with a hedge to the left, go over another stile in the corner and bear gently right to reach a pond and a farm at North Clays. Keeping the farm on your right, join a clear track (over yet another stile!) which goes right (westward) along the right edge of a field. Maintain this course across three fields in all and then cross a dirt road and head into woodland. On emerging into a large field, go half-left and make for a copse. Now go half-right and up to reach a line of trees. At the left end of the trees are a gate and stile: cross and strictly make your way along the right edge of the next field (heading due west). Cross a bridleway and then descend, with a field edge to the left. Go over a stile and walk along the right edge of three fields to join a lane just south of Grove Farm. Follow the lane back to School Lane, then keep ahead to reach the start in Ashurst Wood village.

POINTS OF INTEREST:
The whole of this walk is enjoyable with fine views across valleys north towards Hammerwood House (named for the Sussex iron industry) and, later, southwards across the Medway valley near Cansiron Lane.

REFRESHMENTS:
The Red Barn Inn, Ashurst Wood, but none en route.

Walk 82   WADHURST AND BEWL WATER   7m (11km)

Maps: OS Sheets Landranger 188; Pathfinder 1249.
Woodland paths and the water's edge.
Start: At 641318, Wadhurst Church.

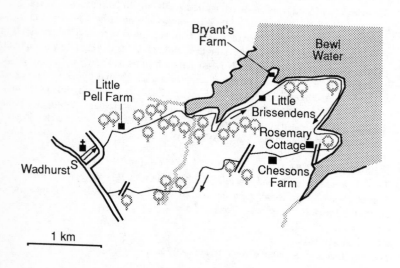

The walk starts in the churchyard of St Peter and St Paul, Wadhurst. Walk to the right of the building to exit by a 'No Cycling' sign. After 400 yards turn right in to a lane and, after a further 400 yards, turn left as the lane bends right, to go along the access drive to Little Pell Farm. The route now heads generally east and north-east, descending through pastures and woodland to reach **Bewl Water**. Turn right and take the clear path, sometimes at the very edge of the reservoir, sometimes a little inland, following waymarks for almost a mile to reach a notice warning you of the angler's priority. Here, turn right, away from the water, passing the buildings and pond of Little Brissendens. Turn left after passing Bryant's House to go along the Private Road towards Bryant's Farm but after about 300 yards go right, along a path which goes down to reach the reservoir again.

Follow the shoreline, for almost 2 miles, eastwards at first then southwards into a wide creek. Now take a westerly path, going through a gate and on to a lane. Turn right for 200 yards, then when just short of Rosemary Cottage, take the footpath to the left. Go along the right edge of two fields to reach Chesson's Farm. Continue through the buildings and along the drive to reach a lane. Turn left for 250 yards, then turn right through a gate and head for the tall, slender spire of Wadhurst Church. Follow the deep grassy track down, soon going between banks to reach a bridge. Cross and continue uphill, and a little right, to reach Little Whiligh. Go through a gate and turn left along a concrete road. After about 500 yards, look out for steps to the right, and descend these to reach a kissing-gate. Go through and continue to descend, with a hedge and fence to the right. Halfway down the hill, go half-left, away from the hedge, heading due west through trees and bracken, making for a little bridge over a stream. Cross and go up to the corner of the next field (with the stream on your left for a while). Climb steadily away from the stream to cross into the next field and continue to reach a narrow lane at the top. Cross two stiles and bear diagonally left across the next field to emerge on to the Wadhurst – Ticehurst road (the B2099). Turn right and follow the road back into Wadhurst.

POINTS OF INTEREST:
Wadhurst – This attractive village was once an iron-mining centre, producing agricultural tools and implements of all kinds. The church has at least thirty iron memorials (ledgers) set in the floor. Note also the modern iron-work, the cross, candlesticks and screen (with lambs, hops and flowers).

Bewl Water – It is possible to walk all around the 15 mile perimeter of the reservoir, but that walk would include a good deal of boring road work. The Reservoir is the largest man-made expanse of water in Sussex, holding 6,900 million gallons. It is 97 feet at its deepest point.

REFRESHMENTS:
The White Hart Inn, Wadhurst.
There are also other possibilities in Wadhurst.

Walk 83   **ALFRISTON**   7½m (12km)

Maps: OS Sheets Landranger 199; Pathfinder 1324.

Quiet downland, a very attractive village and a riverbank. Plus one very steep climb.

Start: At 502005, a lay-by on Alfriston Road, north of Seaford.

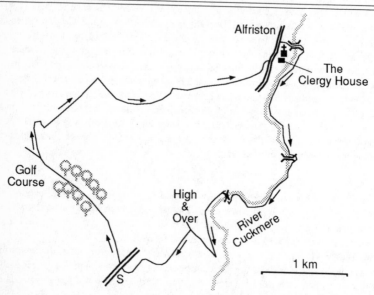

The lay-by is on the right of the road as we leave Seaford's housing area. Walk north, away from Seaford, cross the road and turn left on to a broad track which soon runs between open fields. Continue for ⅔ mile (1km) - skylarks are sure to accompany you – until a hedgerow appears to the left. Go on a further 50 yards on to a track between high hedges. This is known as The Comp. Look out for a sign, to the left by a gate, warning about golfers, and shortly after take a right fork steeply downhill – there is a blue bridleway marker – to reach the valley bottom. Go through a gate on the right with heavy iron weights, and walk for 25 yards to reach a post. Turn right, then left uphill alongside fields and hedges. Go through another weighted gate and walk straight uphill to reach the top of the ridge. Now turn right, with a fence to the left, enjoying views over Newhaven and Seaford. Head half-right, with **Cuckmere**

Haven ahead and **Windover Hill** and The Weald to the left. At the second gate, turn half-left and descend downhill, ignoring all side tracks. Look out left across the fields: llamas can often be seen grazing here. Pass a camp site, tennis courts and a cottage before emerging on to a busy road at Dean's Place, **Alfriston**. Cross and turn left to follow the road to the attractive but often crowded village.

Take the lane on the right, opposite 'Sally's' and the Post Office, down to the Cuckmere river. Turn right, (the church and **Clergy House** may now be visited by crossing the green, to the right) cross the white bridge and turn right over a stile to reach the river bank. Walk along the bank, with the church and Clergy House on the opposite bank, going over several stiles. Ignore the next bridge but after another $^1/_2$ mile (800 metres) cross the second one and continue in the same direction as before. Ahead now, high on the hillside on the right flank of the steep hill is a faintly-etched white horse. About 500 yards on from the bridge the river bends away left. Go forward here, going under the steep hill, and its horse, on a faint path. When approaching a little footbridge, to the left, and an iron gate ahead, look for, and take, a stepped path going right and up the steep pitch of **High and Over**. It is a demanding 300 foot climb but the views at the very top are well worth it. At the top there are a picnic site, explanatory notice and compass rose. Retrace your steps a few yards, downhill, but then turn sharp right below a hedge. Go over several stiles to reach the field hedge in the distance. At the field corner, turn right over a stile by a gate and walk with the field hedge to the left. Keep to the hedge as it turns left, and at the bottom turn right along the road to reach the starting lay-by.

POINTS OF INTEREST:

Cuckmere Haven – The river meets the sea unspoilt by any building – a very rare thing!

Windover Hill – On the summit are prehistoric burials and traces of ancient field farming. 'The Long Man' is on the north facing slope, not visible from this walk.

Alfriston – The church of St Andrew's is often called 'The Cathedral of the Downs'.

The Clergy House – This 14th century half-timbered, thatched house was the first ever purchase of the National Trust – in 1891 for £10.

High and Over – Take the very short detour to enjoy the view and glean interesting information set out on a panoramic board.

REFRESHMENTS:

The complete range is available in Alfriston – from a £25 dinner to a 'pie and a pint' in several fine inns. There are also some tea shops.

Walk 84   **Bo-Peep and Bishopstone**   7$\frac{1}{2}$m (12km)

Maps: OS Sheets Landranger 198 and 199; Pathfinder 1308.

Deep downland valleys and ridges.

Start: At 494050, the car park on the South Downs Way near Selmeston.

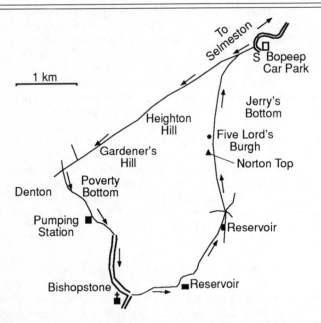

The walk begins at the car park 400 feet above Bo-peep Farm, which is near Selmeston on the A27.

From the car park return a few yards back along the tarmac and turn left through a gate. Follow a track that continues clearly in a south-westerly direction, with a fence to the right. After about $\frac{1}{2}$ mile ($\frac{3}{4}$km) a cattle pen is reached to the left. Go through a gate here, and turn right along another fence. After 50 yards go through a wired gate (not round to the right) and proceed diagonally downhill across a large field (sometimes in crop but the path should be clear) towards a gate. Go through and walk straight ahead, maintaining the same direction and climbing up Heighton Hill by going alongside the fence on the left. Go through another gate at the summit and then along the right-hand edge of the next field. As this field ends, continue with the fence, going round to the left and over a stile. Now walk over the shoulder of Gardener's Hill, with gorse and a fence on the left. Ignoring tracks to the right, descend quite steeply before climbing up again and continuing straight ahead. The tracks here are carved deep in the chalk: as you near the summit, take the one to the left which descends into a valley, Poverty Bottom. Walk for about a mile ($1\frac{1}{2}$kms) along the valley, with a very steep slope to the right, and go past a pumping station, also to the right. It can be very muddy here, though when the track becomes metalled the poverty is somewhat relieved! Continue through the hamlet of Norton, following the lane a further $\frac{3}{4}$ mile ($1\frac{1}{4}$kms) to **Bishopstone** where the church deserves a visit.

As the 'main road' turns southwards and seawards, turn left (due east) on to a wide track and follow it uphill for 400 yards. When the main track turns right, keep left on a grassy path, going over a stile and along the side of a hill, with hedges to the right and a steep slope to the left. Continue in the same direction for another $\frac{1}{2}$ mile ($\frac{3}{4}$kms), passing a reservoir, to the right and, later, walking parallel with a concrete track. Soon a bridleway joins from the right and you pass to the left of another reservoir. Very shortly after, the track joins up with several others: keep straight ahead, on the 'high road' which is leading generally northwards. This is a splendid ridgeway, passing Norton Top, the tumuli of **Five Lord's Burgh** (were five ancient kings buried here?) and – deep and to the right – the curiously named Jerry's Bottom. After a little over $1\frac{1}{2}$ miles we find the cattle pen of the outward journey and, very soon, the car park and starting point.

POINTS OF INTEREST:

Bishopstone – The church has Saxon remains, a Norman arched doorway and a sundial over the porch entrance inscribed Eadric.

Five Lord's Burgh – This is one of the many hundred 'tumuli' which are to be found on the Sussex Downs. They were the burial mounds of our early ancestors. Almost all have been desecrated and dug up for 'treasure' – much of which can now be seen in local museums.

REFRESHMENTS:

Please take your own, there is nothing available en route, and the Downs are very dry!

Walk 85   **BROAD OAK** $7^1/_2$m (12km)

Maps: OS Sheets Landranger 198; Pathfinder 1270 & 1269.

An undulating but gentle country walk with fine views.

Start: At 623237, Paine's Corner in Swiffe Lane, north of the A265.

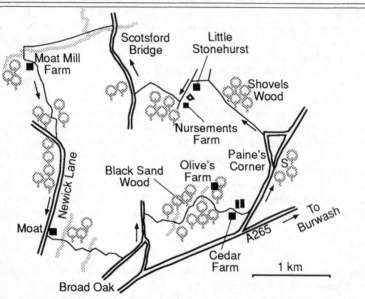

Swiffe Lane leads north-east from the A265: walk along it for $^1/_2$ mile (about 1km) to reach a junction of lanes at Paine's Corner. Continue northwards for a further 400 yards and then, as the lane turns right, bear left. Just short of Pedlar's Cottage, turn right through a wooden gate into a field and go downhill to the left corner where here is a metal fence. Go over, and descend to a footbridge. Cross and maintain direction (north-west) as you go downhill to enter Shovels Wood, with a pond to the left. At the wood's far end, cross a fence and two fields, using a stile between them, to reach a footbridge in the valley. Cross, and go left, and over a stile in a hedge to reach another footbridge. Cross and go uphill towards trees and a pond. Pass the pond on your right to reach a gate left of Little Stonehurst. Turn left along a clear track for 400 yards, to reach Nursement's Farm and go right there to cross a field to a hedge gap to the left of

162

a pond. Now descend, aiming to the left of some trees, to cross a stream. Now go a little to the right and ascend with a hedge to the left, to reach a stile at the top of the field. Cross and continue to another stile. Go over, then on through a gate on to a lane.

Turn right and follow the lane to Scotsford Bridge. Cross, and after another 25 yards, cross the stile to the left and follow the stream, also to the left, for almost a mile (about 1½ kms) using stiles and footbridges to link the fields along this pleasant little valley. In due course a gate appears, to the left. Go through and head southwards leading into Moat Mill Farm. Go through a small wooden gate near a walled garden on the right to reach a stile some 20 yards ahead. Cross, walk another 30 yards and then turn right through a gate. Ascend with a hedge on the right to reach another gateway in the top right field corner. Now make for a stile at the left end of the trees ahead, and go over into a wooded area. After leaving the wood, go along a field with a hedge to the left to reach an iron gate. Go through and turn right along an access drive, ignoring Bungehurst Farm to emerge into Newick Lane. Turn left, and follow the lane for ¾ mile (1¼ kms). Go past Moat Cottage, on the left, and turn left through a gate. The route now heads eastwards, with a hedge to the right. Go downhill into a wood, cross a little stream and go half-right, uphill. Cross a field, go through a gate and then walk downhill once more to cross another stream by footbridge.

Continue along the path beyond the bridge, passing Blackdown Cottage and going up the lane ahead. Turn right and walk to a junction. Turn left and walk forward to the next junction and there turn left again, going downhill. At the end of the first field on the right, take the uphill track to walk past a wood. When this track curves left, go into the wood, Black Sand Wood, and walk north-east to reach a barn by Olive's Farm. Keep right through the farm, then go across a field and into a copse. On the far side of the copse, take the left path fork down to a footbridge. Cross and continue to reach some greenhouses, passing between them and Cedar Swiffe Farm, and continuing to reach a lane. Turn left along the lane to return to the start at Paine's Corner.

POINTS OF INTEREST:

The chief joys of this walk through the Sussex Weald are the little things – busy farmers, sparkling streams, wild flowers and birds.

At nearby Heathfield one of Britain's earliest natural gas supplies was discovered, accidentally, by water engineers in 1895. At one time the supply provided 15 million cubic feet of gas each day.

REFRESHMENTS:

At Broad Oak and Heathfield, but not en route.

Walk 86 ERIDGE STATION AND CROWBOROUGH 7¹/₂m (12km)

Maps: OS Sheets Landranger 188; Pathfinder 1248.

Along the rim of a valley and back along it, north-east of Crowborough.

Start: At 542345, Eridge Station, between Crowborough and Tunbridge Wells.

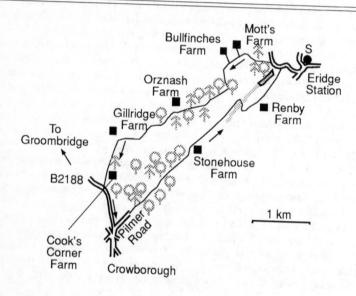

From the railway station, cross Hamsell Bridge on the A26, heading south. On the far side of the bridge, turn right along the lane which runs parallel to the railway, following it as it bends left, right and right again. Leave the lane by taking the access drive to Mott's and Bullfinches Farms, but do not turn right into either. Instead, continue south-west and then west to reach a footbridge. Continue ahead along the valley's rim, often walking in woodland, to reach the buildings and ivy covered oast of Orznash Farm. Maintain direction, with fine views across the valley, to reach Gillridge Farm. Now join the tree-lined drive to Stonecroft Farm, then go left, downhill through Tyler's Wood to reach the main B2188.

164

Turn left and follow the road with care. After 400 yards, turn left into Pilmer Road – refreshments are available in central **Crowborough** ahead. The lane becomes rougher, finally becoming a track into woodland. Continue along the track for almost a mile to reach Stonehouse Farm. Here, go through a gate and pass a cottage to the left. Go over a stile by another gate and then walk with a hedge to the left and, soon, woodland to the right. Follow the direction of a stream down on the right to reach a very large field. Go directly across this, or around the right edges by the stream in the valley bottom. Maintain direction to reach a pond. Go through a gate to the left of a clear track and walk along a field beyond. As this field narrows to a point, go through a gap in the hedge then bear right, cross the stream and ascend for some 300 yards. At a junction of tracks, turn left for another 350 yards. The way now appears to be right, leading to Renby Farm, do not go that way: instead, keep straight on, through crops if necessary, making for the right-hand corner of the wood ahead. On reaching this, keep ahead alongside the coniferous woods to the left. Go over a low railing and continue to the drive from Hamsell Lake House. Follow this to a lane. A right turn now takes us back to Eridge Station and the start.

POINTS OF INTEREST:

Crowborough – The town was once a centre for iron-smelting (and smuggling!) and was advertised as 'The Scotland of Sussex' at the turn of the century because of the hills and the adjacent commons of Ashdown Forest. Sir Arthur Conan Doyle, the creator of Sherlock Holmes, lived and died at Windlesham Manor, near the golf course. He was at first buried in his garden, but his remains were later moved to the family vault. All this gave rise to rumours that the place was haunted so it was exorcised! Beacon House is the highest inhabited building in Sussex, at 796 feet above sea level.

REFRESHMENTS;

The Huntsman Inn, Eridge.
The Nevil Crst and Gun Inn, Eridge.
A wide range of choices are also available in Crowborough.

Walk 87   BODIAM CASTLE   8m (13km)

Maps: OS Sheets Landranger 199; Pathfinder 1270.

The old hop-gardens of north-east Sussex, a few yards into Kent and a picture-book castle.

Start: At 783254, the Castle car park, Bodiam.

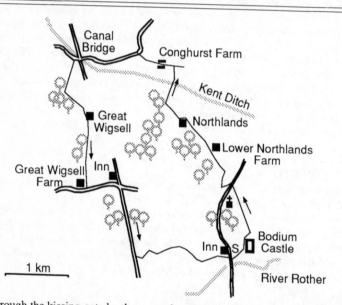

Go through the kissing-gate by the car park and climb the little hill near the trees to reach the moated, crenellated manor of **Bodiam Castle**. Pass the front of the kiosk and Museum (a visit, plus photographs, will add an hour of pleasure to the walk) and use the stile and footpath to reach another stile, continuing on to reach Court Lodge Farm. Keep to the right of the buildings, and go straight over a crossing track. Now walk down, keeping left of a white house, and go through a gate on to a road. Go right, then left along a lane to Lower Northlands Farm. Go through a gate on the left, and along the hedge to the right, to reach Northlands Farm. Keep left behind the buildings, then go right, descending and going between woodland to reach the Kent Ditch. The metal bridge (made with metal from a World War II aircraft transporter) takes you over the Ditch into Kent.

Continue uphill for 500 yards, then go left beside an orchard, to the right, to reach Conghurst Farm. Continue ahead to reach a lane. Go left along the lane to reach Canal Bridge and the A229. Cross, with care, to the road opposite and, shortly, go left into a lane running due south and back into East Sussex. Climb the hill ahead towards the left edge of a wood, and then bear left and down to Great Wigsell. A right and a left turn through the buildings brings you to a footpath heading due south. Go across two fields and alongside the wood to the left to reach Great Wigsell Farm. Continue ahead to reach a lane, and turn left to a crossroads and the CurlewInn. Turn right, along the A229, walking carefully for $^1/_2$ mile ($^3/_4$kms) and looking out for a footpath on the left that crosses a field towards Bodiam. The path winds gently, veering and then running parallel to the River Rother, as it crosses five fields to reach the Castle Inn, Bodiam. It is now just a short stroll back to the start.

POINTS OF INTEREST:

Bodiam Castle – The castle was built began in 1385 as part of the defensive system against the threat of invasion from France but no battle was ever fought here. The castle was slighted – made useless as a fortress – by General Waller's Parliamentarian army during the Civil War, but is still virtually intact, with its beautiful moat, it is now the almost perfect 'fairy-tale' castle. The museum contains finds made during the excavation of the site.

Elsewhere in Bodiam, the railway station is also of historical interest, while across the river you can try the 'rural experience' at Quarry Farm. Although mainly for children (with pigs, bee-keeping, sheep-shearing, etc. plus steam rollers), there is also much for adults to enjoy.

REFRESHMENTS:

The Curlew Inn, on the route.
The Castle Inn, Bodiam.
There are also other possibilities in Bodiam, and at the castle.

Walk 88　　JACK, JILL AND KEYMER　　8m (13km)

Maps: OS Sheets Landranger 198; Pathfinder 1288.

A walk along the East-West Sussex Border.

Start: At 301134, the Jack and Jill (Mill Lane) car park, near Clayton.

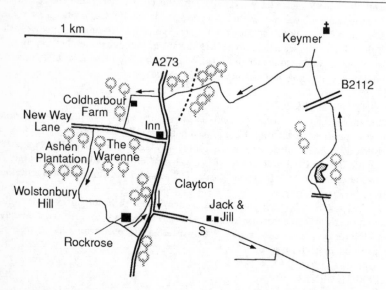

This walk can readily be combined with Walk 38 to make a splendid day's outing.

From the **Jack and Jill** car park proceed uphill, passing the mills on your left. In about a mile, after having joined the South Downs Way, you will come to Keymer Post. Some 20 yards beyond the new acorn post, go left through a gate and descend, heading due north along the top of a bank. Near the bottom, as the clear track curves right, take a narrower path, going through a bushy area to reach a lane. Cross the lane and go over the stile opposite. Now take the path alongside the pond on the right, heading north-eastwards, for 400 yards to reach a second lane. Turn left along the lane to reach the B2112 by Lodge Farm, to the right. Cross into Lodge Lane and maintain the northerly direction to reach houses on the outskirts of **Keymer** village. Just before Number 42 go left over a stile and cross the field beyond, heading south-westwards. Keep on clear paths for about $^2/_3$ mile (1 km) to reach a lonely house. Turn right and go over a cattle grid. Now turn left, cross a stile and go right across a grassy field. Keep left at a fork and continue ahead to cross a bridge over the railway. The generally westward direction is now maintained along a clear footpath which reaches the A273. Cross, with care, and turn right for about 25 yards and then go left into a field. Keep along the field's right edge to reach a second field. Go left, southwards, through Coldharbour Farm, continuing for about 250 yards to reach New Way Lane. (At this junction a left turn will take you to the Jack and Jill Inn.) Turn right and after 300 yards go left and steeply uphill along the chalk 'bostal', with Ashen plantation on the right and The Warenne on the left. Keep ahead along Wellcombe Bottom below Wolstonbury Hill and when the path climbs more steeply, go left through a gate on to a path through woods. At a signed cross-path, turn right, going steeply uphill to reach a stile on to open downland. Soon, go left over another stile, then turn right into an enclosed track. Turn left shortly, just above the Rockrose Farm buildings. Fork left on to a track which leads into the farmyard and cross a stile by a gate. You are now walking northwards and parallel to the very busy A273: the way is somewhat indistinct, going through scrub, bushes and trees – Clayton Tunnel is under your feet – to reach a stile. Cross and descend through more trees to reach a road. Great care is required now, as you walk about 200 yards uphill to reach Mill Lane, to the left. Turn left into the lane to reach the starting point near the mills.

POINTS OF INTEREST:

Jack and Jill – Jill, the white building, is a post mill once sited at Patcham, north of Brighton and brought over the Downs by oxen. Now restored, the mill is open on Sunday afternoons. Jack is a brick tower mill.

Keymer – The church has an unusual dedication – to two Arabian, Eastern Orthodox churchmen, Saint Cosmas and Saint Damian, the patron saints of doctors.

REFRESHMENTS:

The Jack & Jill Inn, requiring a short detour near Coldharbour Farm.
There are also possibilities in Keymer and Hassocks.

Walk 89 MOUNTFIELD AND THE DARWELL RESERVOIR 8m (13km)

Maps: OS Sheets Landranger 199; Pathfinder 1270.
Woods, pastures, crops and views, six miles north of Battle.
Start: At 734203, Mountfield Church.

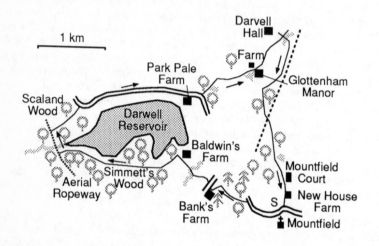

Set off from the church in a westerly direction, going along the lane for about 500
yards. When the lane bends right, go ahead on a track through woods. Keep right at a
fork to emerge into a field. Maintain direction over a stile and continue into a second
wood, still heading westwards. Cross a little bridge and another stile to emerge into
fields again. Ascend, go through a gate and turn left into a little lane. Walk along this
for 25 yards, then go right into another small wood. Continue ahead, going out into a
field and soon passing to the left of Baldwin's Farm. Go through the gate in the
corner, then diagonally left across the next field. Go through another gate and keep
ahead, with a fence at first, on the right, then on the left. You will soon pick up a
signpost and waymarks that help you through the trees. Another gate and field lie
ahead as you make for Simmett's Wood. Walk through this fine woodland, staying

near the southern edge of **Darwell Reservoir**, but never having access to it. A mile of walking brings you to the **aerial ropeway** which carries gypsum from the local mines.

Careful now: cross the track and go half-right for 20 yards to reach a second track. Turn right along this (the ropeway is now above), then go left towards a 'cage'. Take the path to the right just before reaching the cage, going into Scaland Wood, and heading north-eastwards to reach a lane. Go right and follow the lane eastwards, admiring the views of the reservoir to the right. After passing Park Pale Farm, to the right, the lane bends right: look out for, and take, a path on the left through trees. The path soon comes out into fields again. Keep north-eastwards to pass to the right of the moat of Glottenham Castle and continue to reach Glottenham Farm's oast and Manor. Now begin heading more northerly, going along a good track. When you are level with Darwell Hall, to the left, turn right along a path heading eastwards to reach the railway line. Bear right and follow the line, going over streams and through a little wood to reach a bridge under the railway. Go under, cross the field beyond and through a gate. Now bear right, ascending to reach more trees. Pass to the left of these and keep up the hill ahead, passing a pond, to reach a gate at the top. Go through the gate and along the path beside Mountfield Court to reach a drive. Turn right, along this, passing New House Farm and continuing to reach the road near the start. To return to the church, turn right along the road.

POINTS OF INTEREST:

Darwell Reservoir – The water covers 170 acres of farmland that was dammed and flooded in 1950. In droughts the remnants of another Sussex iron furnace can be seen.

Aerial Ropeway – Gypsum is extracted from the mines nearby. An aerial ropeway – which passes over the walk – connects the mines to the loading area from where the mineral is transported to be used in cement making, dental moulds and plasterboard manufacture.

REFRESHMENTS:

None en route, so it's picnic and flasks!

Walk 90 BOREHAM STREET, HOOE AND WARTLING 8m (13km)

Maps: OS Sheets Landranger 199; Pathfinders 1290 and 1309.

An easy walk by Pevensey Levels and farmland.

Start: At 666113, in Boreham Street on the A271 between Ninfield and Herstmonceux.

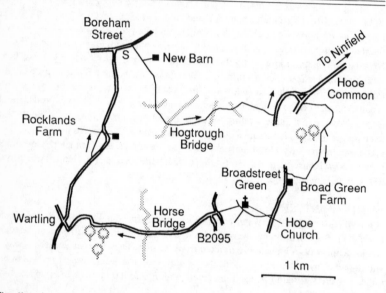

The directions for this walk are deliberately not quite so detailed, allowing the walker to use common-sense (and compass?) to complete an interesting circuit. Almost half the distance covered is along lanes, so extra care is required.

From the straggly village of **Boreham Street** walk along the busy A271, with care, for a short distance, then turn right on to the track and access to New Barn. After about 200 yards, bear right (SSW) descending across fields for a further 600 yards to cross a stream. Keeping right of another brook (all these brooks are draining the flat **Pevensey Levels**), continue and cross the wider Waller's Haven at Hogtrough(!) Bridge. Turn left and walk due east to reach another bridge. There, turn right to reach a third bridge near power lines. The easterly course is now maintained, going uphill for another 600 yards to reach a road. Turn left, and follow the road around a bend and into Hooe Common.

At the fork, keep right (refreshments at hand) and go right again at the junction. After a few yards continue your easterly way, going across fields for 400 yards to reach a T-junction of footpaths. Turn right here, taking the path that heads due south. After keeping to the right edge of a field, you will reach a fork. Keep right again, and walk diagonally across a field. Go across the right corner of the next field, by some trees. Now maintain the southwards course, walking alongside fields. Ignore an access lane to the right by buildings, but soon bear right, westwards, before reaching Broad Green Farm to reach a lane and the hamlet of Broad Street Green. Turn left along the lane, going through the hamlet to reach a footpath on the right. Follow this, keeping to the right side of the fields to reach the lonely Hooe church of **St Oswald's**. From the church, maintain the westerly course to reach a road junction. With care, cross the B2095, continue to head west, on a lane which descends to cross Waller's Haven (again) at Horse Bridge. Continue along the lane, ascending to the village of **Wartling**.

The route continues by going first right on a lane signed to Boreham Street. The lane can be followed all the way to the start, but it is possible to cut off a corner by using a field path to the left, about a mile from Wartling, just before Rocklands Farm. When the A271 is reached, turn right to return to the start.

POINTS OF INTEREST:

St Oswald's Church, Hooe – The church is remotely set in fields. The chancel is set at an angle to the nave to represent the angle of Christ's head on the cross. Inside there is a rood screen with stone supports.

Wartling – The village church, dedicated to St Mary Magdalene, has at least two unusual features, a royal coat of arms and a carved wooden heron supporting the lectern.

Pevensey Levels – The Levels are 11,000 acres of wetlands and are designated as a Site of Special Scientific Interest. It was once a tidal marsh, or perhaps even under the sea, but has been reclaimed by the digging of miles of drainage ditches and 'havens' and is now good agricultural soil. In the 11th century Pevensey Castle was on the coast, but now it is a mile inland. The Levels offer good chances of seeing a number of marsh birds.

REFRESHMENTS:

The King's Arms, Hooe Common.
The Lamb Inn, Wartling.
There are also possibilities in Boreham Street.

Walk 91 THE GUN, COGGER'S AND THE CUCKOO 8m (13km)

Maps: OS Sheets Landranger 199; Pathfinder 1289.

Part of The Wealdway, much of the Cuckoo Walk and a charming churchyard.

Start: At 565146, Gun Hill, off the A22 north of Boship Roundabout.

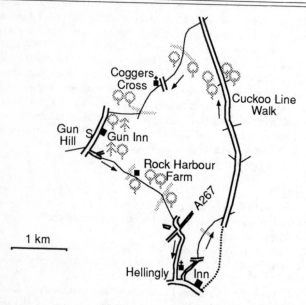

Walk south from the Gun Inn and turn left along the lane signed 'Coggers Cross'. After 250 yards, keep right along the access drive to Rock Harbour Farm. At the farm, fork right past the pond and farmhouse, and then look for and cross a stile with Wealdway waymarks, up in the hedge to the left. With farm buildings to the left, go forward over two stiles and keep ahead to the far left field corner. Follow the hedge to the left, then cross two more stiles and walk along the right edge of the next field. Soon, further Wealdway signs give the direction into a little wood and over two streams. Ascend and, maintaining the generally southerly course, cross a drive and a stile, then go down steps to reach a road. Turn right to join the busy A267.

Cross, with care, and after a few yards turn left into a lane and follow it down to **Hellingly Church** with its adjacent cottages. At the north-east corner of the churchyard, go left along a lane to reach a junction. Fork right, and then take the footpath, to the left, near the buildings. Go along the left edge of three fields to reach a cross track. Go ahead, crossing the corner of the next field to meet the **Cuckoo Walk**.

The 'refreshment alternative' from the churchyard is to leave at the south-east corner, going along a lane for 500 yards to reach the Golden Martlet Inn. The Cuckoo Walk can now be reached by going along the right edge of the car park and turning left along a disused railway line. About 1 mile to the north you will reach the main walk again.

Continue along the old line, ignoring all other access points. About $\frac{1}{2}$ mile after passing a disused brickworks, to the right, leave the Walk by going left, over a stile, into the left corner of a small paddock. Now head south-westward along the left edge of three fields and then go down to reach a stream in woodland. The path now goes a little left, crosses the stream, then goes right and up to cross a field to its top left corner. Go along the left edge of two more fields, then under power lines to reach a stile. Go over on to the access drive of Coggers Farm. Keep heading south-westwards, going along the drive to reach a road at Coggers Cross. Cross the road and follow the lane opposite downhill to Swansbrook Farm, to the left. Now turn right along a bridleway, with woods on both sides, to reach a road. Turn left to return to the Gun Inn and Gun Hill.

POINTS OF INTEREST:

This walk, like all the others, has so many things to savour: the ever-changing clouds; the seasonal round of farming with crops sown, grown and harvested; the birds and their songs; the beauty of wild flowers; the distant views; the shape and colour of trees; the fungi, the old cottages and churches; the association with past inhabitants both famous and 'ordinary' – all add to the physical enjoyment of walking in East Sussex . Don't miss them – they are there for you to see.

Hellingly Church – The church has Norman origins, but was much restored in 1869. The oval churchyard plus the delightful cottages are also to be admired.

The Cuckoo Walk – This footpath, cycle track and bridleway from Polegate to Heathfield follows an old railway line (the Cuckoo Line). It is decorated with specially commissioned sculptures and can be busy during summer weekends.

REFRESHMENTS:

The Gun Inn, Gun Hill.
The Golden Martlet, Hellingly.

Walk 92   **THE LONG MAN OF WILMINGTON**   8½m (14km)
Maps: OS Sheets Landranger 199; Pathfinder 1324.
A mystery carving and a heathland stroll.
Start: At 559038, Folkington Church.

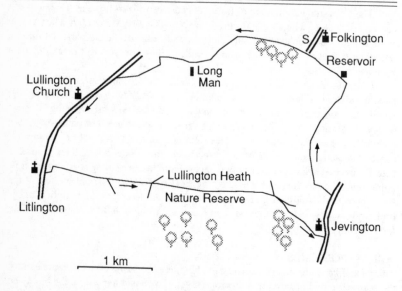

Park carefully at **Folkington Church** and walk forward into a wood-enclosed area.
Turn right along a clear path heading westward following it along the edge of woodland.
This part of the walk follows the Wealdway long distance footpath, for about ½ mile
(¾kms). Do not descend at the right fork which goes down towards the church: instead,
keep left and go up through a gate. Now carry straight on. The hills to the left are
topped by a long barrow burial and some smaller tumuli and, in due course, **The Long
Man** himself appears. Detour left along a clear track if you wish to examine him more
closely. After a further mile (about 1½kms), go through a gate and turn left, uphill.
After a further 80 – 100 yards, descend to reach a clear chalk track and follow it to a
road. With care, turn left along the road passing **Lullington Church** on your right.
Continue along the road to reach the pretty village of Litlington. The pub and tearooms
are ahead, but the route takes a path through a farmyard almost opposite the church.

Turn left, and then right, into a stony, and sometimes muddy, lane. Go uphill, and then straight on, ignoring all branchlines and other tracks, to cross two ridges of Lullington Heath Nature Reserve to reach Old Kiln Bottom. The route now passes through a wood – you are now on a second long distance path, the South Downs Way – before turning right, then left, downhill. Go through the churchyard to reach a road at Jevington. Turn left, walking past the pub and 'Old Post Office' and then turning left on to a rough track leading to the foot of the hill ahead. There, a Wealdway sign directs you to an enclosed bridleway. Continue steadily along this chalky path, keeping roughly to the same contour. Go past a reservoir, to the right, before curving left to return to Folkington.

POINTS OF INTEREST:

Folkington Church – Note the box pews, the monument to Mrs Woodhouse and that to Viscount Monckton who lived nearby and advised the young King Edward VIII during the controversial days of the Abdication.

The Long Man – At 227 feet tall, and once cut into the chalk, but now marked with 700 painted stones, the Long Man is a mystery. Did he appear in the Bronze Age, is he King Harold (1066 and all that), a Roman soldier, a God of Fertility? Nobody knows. All that is known for sure is that this is probably the world's largest depiction of a human figure.

Lullington Church – At sixteen feet square the church has a strong claim to being the smallest in England. It is actually what remains of a medieval building and is well worth a very small detour. Services are held regularly.

REFRESHMENTS:

The Plough and Harrow, Litlington.
The Eight Bells Inn, Jevington.
There is also a tearoom in Litlington.

Walk 93   LEWES, RODMELL AND IFORD   8½m (14km)

Maps: OS Sheets Landranger 198; Pathfinder 1308.
The bank of the Ouse and two villages south of Lewes.
Start: At 412096, near Southover Church, Lewes.

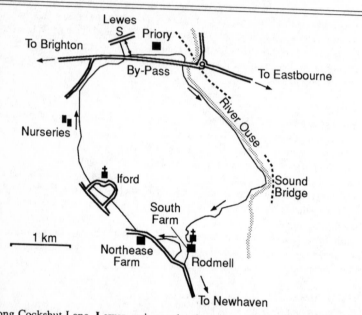

Go along Cockshut Lane, **Lewes,** going under the railway tunnel and then turning left. Pass the Old Priory and some cottages, to the right, turn left along a lane and almost immediately go right and walk to an iron gate. Go through and walk past the household waste area. Now turn right along the bank of the River Ouse going under the new Lewes bypass. Follow the river for 2 miles (3kms) as it winds seawards. After passing a railway bridge (Sound Bridge) on the far side, the river takes a long left bend: stay on the bank, but just before Asham Wharf turn right at a concrete sign and proceed along a track into the village of **Rodmell**. Go up the main street, passing Monk's House, then turn left into the churchyard. Keep to the right to cross the wall and go through South Farm beyond to reach the main Newhaven to Lewes road.

Turn right, and after 200 yards turn right again to go back into the village. Before reaching the church, turn left by a concrete sign (there is a school sign on the right

178

side of the road). Go through a small gate, over a stile and across the field beyond to reach a road. Bear right along the road for about 400 yards to reach some cottages, to the right, and Northease Farm, to the left. Turn right here following the waymarks 'To Iford and Lewes', going over several stiles and gates. When a lane is reached a short detour can be made by turning right to visit St Nicholas' Church, **Iford**. Continue along the lane to rejoin the waymarked path – now signed to Swanborough and Lewes. Turn right along the waymarked path, but just before a gate and stile leading out on to the Newhaven to Lewes road, go half-right along a stream. Go through several gates to reach a point where the stream enters a culvert-pipe. Nearby is the bridge underpass, beneath the Lewes bypass, taken earlier in the walk. Now reverse the outward route to return to Cockshut Lane and the church where the walk started.

POINTS OF INTEREST:

Lewes – The Priory of St Pancras was completed late in the 11th century and lasted until Henry VIII dissolved the monasteries. Then, most of the stones were used for other buildings in the vicinity. The founders, William de Warenne and his wife Gundreda were buried here, their caskets having been discovered in 1845 and re-buried in Southover Church beneath a black marble tombstone found at nearby Isfield (See also the Note to Walk 34).

Rodmell – A village of thatch, flint and half-timbered homes, with a Norman church. Monk's House was the home of Leonard and Virginia Woolf. In 1941 Virginia, severely depressed, walked down the lane and drowned herself. Leonard died here in 1969. The house is open on Wednesdays and Saturdays in summer. At South Farm there is an ancient mulberry tree, was used during the 17th century to establish a local silk industry, silkworms being fed on mulberry leaves.

Iford – This almost forgotten village off the main road was a busy fishing-port at a time when the Ouse was wider and more estuarine. Several large houses with a variety of architectural features add to the interest of a tour of the village. The chancel and nave of St Nicholas' Church were not built square and so the tower, which was built afterwards, twists around to manage the odd angles.

REFRESHMENT:

The Abergavenny Arms, Rodmell. In addition to the refreshments on offer, the inn is worth a visit to see the 80 foot deep well in the lounge and roof beams from Spanish Armada ship wrecks.

There are also numerous possibilities in Lewes.

Walk 94 EASTBOURNE'S DOWNLAND AND CLIFF TOPS 9m (14½km)

Maps: OS Sheets Landranger 199; Pathfinder 1324.

A quiet farmland ramble followed by a bracing cliff walk.

Start: At 588978, the Warren Hill car park above Eastbourne.

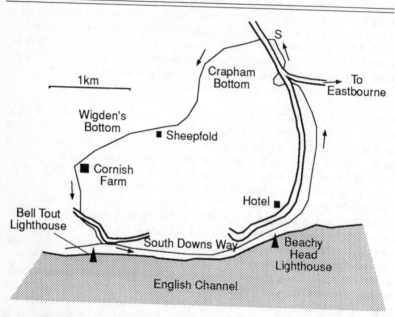

From the car park cross the busy road and go through the gate opposite to descend into the valley 'Crapham Bottom' ahead. Continue through gates and over stiles, passing a dewpond, a sheepfold and a small pump house to reach a fence. Now turn right along the valley, Wigden's Bottom, to reach a gate, another dewpond and a larger, pumping station, on the right. The route continues ahead, going through a double gate and then a bridle gate. Ignore other paths going up to the right, continuing straight on to reach Cornish Farm, which is passed to your left. A few yards past the farm, look for a concrete track leading left, towards the sea and cliffs. Go along this track for about ½ mile (¾kms), heading directly for the **Belle Tout Lighthouse** to reach a road. Turn left along the road, following it around a right-hand curve – please use the grass bank for safety – and the edging off to the right to join the **South Downs Way**

180

on the cliffs. Continue left, that is easterly, in the direction of Eastbourne. The route passes a car park, to the left and **Beachy Head Lighthouse**, below and to the right, to reach the Beachy Head Hotel. Here make for the wide grassy verge, with the road to Eastbourne on the left and the town visible ahead. Across the bay, if visibility permits, it is possible to make out Pevensey, Hastings and Fairlight. About a mile (1$^1/_2$kms), beyond the hotel, a junction of roads is reached. Ignore the road descending, to the right, into the town, and cross to the left. Go uphill, then cross the road again into the Warren Hill car park where the walk began.

POINTS OF INTEREST:

Belle Tout Lighthouse – This disused lighthouse was built of granite in 1631, but was found to be unsatisfactory as it was often shrouded in sea-fret rolling in from the English Channel. As a result, the present day Beachy Head Lighthouse was erected below the cliff.

The South Downs Way – This National Trail was officially opened in July 1972. It has two starts in Eastbourne and ends near Winchester. Much of it follows an ancient trackway used by Stone Age man.

Beachy Head Lighthouse – The beam from the lighthouse can be seen for over 16 miles. The cliffs behind, of Beachy Head itself, rise 534 feet (163 metres) from the sea, the highest sea cliffs in southern England. The cliffs are formed where the South Downs reach the Channel. Before the 1939-45 War, farming on the Downs was almost exclusively sheep-rearing, but the demand for grain changed the face of the area so that there are now many large wire-fenced fields with a variety of crops. The loneliness of the country on this walk is in marked contrast to the busy holiday scene along the roads, promenade and beaches nearby.

REFRESHMENTS:
The Beachy Head Hotel.

LITLINGTON AND JEVINGTON   9m (14½ km)

or 10m (16km)

Maps: OS Sheets Landranger 199; Pathfinder 1324.
A glorious downland walk plus forest tracks and some prehistory.
Start: At 523019, Litlington village.

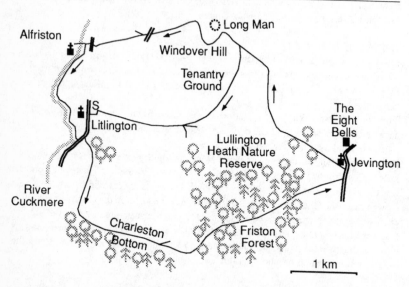

Walk south out of the village of **Litlington** and as the road bends right, turn left uphill to reach a kissing-gate on the right. Go through and up the field ahead to the top left corner. Go over a stile and on to a second stile. You are on the South Downs Way: follow the acorns down to a stile close to Charleston Manor, then go left and keep left along the valley floor. Near the forest ahead, begin to climb half-right across scrub to join a clear track coming in from the right. Follow the track into Friston Forest, soon veering half-left (north-east). Maintain direction for about 1½ miles (2½ kms), ignoring other wide tracks and rides, and staying roughly on the same contour, to emerge above **Jevington**. Continue north-easterly in open country, going downhill to reach a road. Turn left into Jevington. Take a lane on the left to regain the South Downs Way passing St Andrew's Church. To find refreshments, do not turn left, but continue ahead, returning to the church. Go past the churchyard on to an enclosed path, ascending to reach a path junction. Go left with the South Downs Way marker, climbing steeply to reach another junction. The acorns now direct you to the right: head northwards through gates on to open downland and a deep valley, Tenantry Ground, to the left. A track comes up from the left here, before the Way goes through a gate.

For the shorter walk, go sharply left, keeping the valley on the right. Curve south-west until, having passed through gates, a junction of footpaths is reached at Cross Dyke with its tumuli. Go right and descend for about a mile: near the end the track is deep and enclosed. At the bottom, go left to reach farm buildings. When a concrete path is reached, turn right into Litlington village to regain the start.

For the longer walk, go ahead through the gate. You are now above the **Long Man,** though a detour right is necessary for closer observation. Now make a southerly half-circle round the top of **Windover Hill** before descending westwards to pass a reservoir, to the right. Go across a minor road and walk steeply down to Plonk Barn. The alternative South Downs Way route joins us: keep ahead, crossing a stream and a meadow to reach a fine white bridge (to visit Alfriston, *see* Note to Walk 83, cross the bridge). The walk goes left over the stile just before the bridge and continues to follow the Cuckmere river (about $1\frac{1}{2}$ miles) before turning left by a bridge. Follow a track to a gate and go through on to a road. Turn left and follow the road back into Litlington.

POINTS OF INTEREST:

Litlington – St Michael the Archangel Church, built of flint, white weather-boarding and with a shingled spire has Norman origins. It has a 13th century sundial and houses the tomb of the first Lieutenant Governor of Victoria, Australia, the man who suggested to Gladstone, in 1846, that no further convicts be sent to Australia.

Windover Hill and the Long Man – Hereabouts in Neolithic and Bronze Age times early man buried his dead in long and round 'barrows'. The Long Man itself is a chalk cut figure which stands 73 metres high. When the outline was first cut is unknown. Is it pre-Roman, medieval or recent? Historians are still puzzled. What is certain is that man has found the views exceptional for many centuries.

Jevington – St Andrews Church is full of interest : the tower is Saxon, Roman bricks were used to block windows on the north and south walls and there is a tapsell gate incorporating a stile.

REFRESHMENTS:
The Plough & Harrow, Litlington. There is also a tearoom in the village.
The Eight Bells, Jevington.
There are also several places in Alfriston.

Maps: OS Sheets Landranger 199; Pathfinder 1309.
A contrast to Downland or Weald – flat, desolate pastureland.
Start: In Hailsham, 10 miles north of Eastbourne.

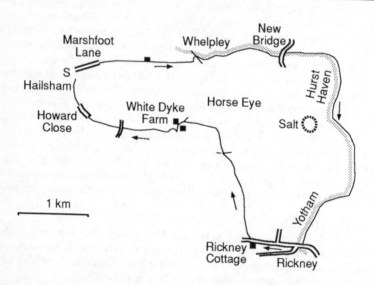

This challenging walk attempts to 'get away from it all' in a silent flat landscape crossed by dozens of drainage ditches with rushes, reeds and much to interest the observer of the flora and fauna of marshland. Some 11,000 acres of the wetlands between Pevensey and Herstmonceux are a 'Site of Special Scientific Interest' and much is protected by the Sussex Trust for Nature Conservation. Extra care is required to navigate across the marshlands: do not attempt this walk after heavy rain.

Begin in busy **Hailsham** at the junction of High Street and George Street. Walk along Vicarage Road into Marshfoot Lane – aptly named after prolonged wet weather. The way is now simply eastward into **Pevensey Levels**, going through gates, walking on top of raised banks and going over footbridges to reach New Bridge and a lane. Turn left and follow the lane as it turns right and left, crossing two bridges. Immediately after the second, turn right, ignoring a half-left footpath to regain an easterly course along the north bank of a large ditch. After a while the ditch widens: follow it southwards. The route is on the left of the ditch, which is called Hurst Haven. Go through several gates and enjoy the view of Herstmonceux Church and the old Royal Observatory buildings to the north-east as you follow the ditch for $2\frac{1}{2}$ miles. In medieval times salt-making was an important industry locally, traces of the trade having been found to the west and south.

The ditch reaches a road at Rickney, a tiny hamlet: turn right, go over a bridge and follow the signpost 'to Hailsham'. Keep westward now, passing Rickney Farm and a lane going north. Shortly after passing Rickney Cottage, to the left, turn right over a rough stile. Go through a gate, then veer left for 20 yards to go through another gate. Now go right, northwards, and maintain this direction with field edges to the right, until you can bear a little to the right to over a bridge in the distant corner of the second field. Turn left with a ditch to reach another bridge. Now keep heading northwards, crossing restored bridges and culverts as you approach the buildings of White Dyke Farm. When a green path is reached, make a firm left turn along it. Hailsham can be seen clearly ahead now: go to the left of the farm buildings and along the farm's access drive. Walk past a caravan site, to the right, to meet a road at a T-junction. Go left, and then immediately right to cross the road into a field. Walk across several fields to reach Howard Close, to the right. At the end of the Close, turn right into Swan Road. Now go left into the busy road that leads to the centre of Hailsham and the start of the walk.

POINTS OF INTEREST:

Hailsham – The town was once an important centre for rope, string, twine and sack-making. In the 19th century it was known locally as 'String Town'. The Heritage Centre, off Market Street, houses many local objects pertaining to local farming, together with industrial relics and a reconstructed Victorian kitchen.

Pevensey Levels – Two thousand years ago much of this area was under water. The Saxons named many of the higher points, using their suffix for 'island', –ey or –eye. Examples are Horse Eye, Langney, Rickney, Pevensey and Glyndley. Some of the area's streams were big enough to allow merchant boats to use them. Since then the Levels have been so well-drained that the area is now rich pastureland, though it remains a haunt for waterbirds. In addition to herons and swans all year, there are redshank, snipe and plovers in the summer. Some rare plants such as water-soldier and water-violet are found here too.

REFRESHMENTS:

There is a variety in Hailsham, but for the rest of the walk you must take it with you!

Walk 98 SILVER HILL AND THE ROTHER VALLEY 10m (16km)
Maps: OS Sheets Landranger 199; Pathfinder 1270.
A long walk along the Rother Valley on the Kent-Sussex border.
Start: At 737261, the White Horse Inn, Silver Hill.

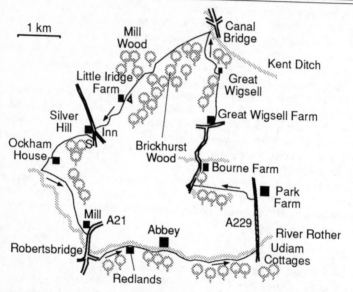

The start is on the A21 about 2 miles (3kms) north of Robertsbridge. Go south from the inn for about 200 yards and take the drive to the right which leads down to Ockham House. After ¾ mile (1¼kms) turn right, between trees and beside a chalet, to pass some garages and a greenhouse, to the left, keep going downhill (it is steep and can be slippery), then turn left by the mill stream. Continue south-east, then south to pass the mill and the race, then go left, over the weir, to reach the A21.

Turn right along the main road then cross, with care, and go left up Fair Lane following it to reach Redlands, to the right. Continue along the lane to reach the remains of the valley's Cistercian Abbey. Go right and left with the lane, then take the stiles to the left, to reach the River Rother. Bear right to follow the river, with two large fields to the right, to reach a brick built gun-house(?) and the A229 at Udiam Cottages.

Turn left along the main road, taking great care. After about $^1/_2$ mile ($^3/_4$kms), as the road climbs, and opposite the entrance to Park Farm, turn half-left and across a field to its left corner. Now walk across the next field, going due west to pass to the right of two ponds, and heading for the right edge of some trees. Go through into the next field and cross to the corner where there is another pond, to the right. Go alongside a copse, to the left, and continue to reach a lane. Turn right, along this quiet lane, passing Bourne Farm, and going over a stream. Continue to a T-junction. Turn right, but soon go left, using the footpath between buildings of Great Wigsell Farm, heading northwards through three fields to reach Great Wigsell. Here, left and right turns take you up to the edge of Brickhurst Wood. Go half-right, downhill, to reach a stream, the Kent Ditch. Turn left just before the stream and walk alongside it to reach a brick bridge. Cross this, go along by the trees to the right for a few yards, then go across a field, making for the corner of Mill Wood. Continue with the wood to the right, then go through the woodland which stretches across the route. Go through a gate and across the field beyond – it was once an orchard – to reach the barns at Little Iridge Farm. Go to the left of these and take the track winding down to the houses and the White Horse Inn on the A21.

POINTS OF INTEREST:

Robertsbridge – The village is famous for cricket bat making, strong wooden toys (made by the Hutterian Brotherhood) and, in medieval days, the fine Cistercian Abbey, the ruins of which are passed on the walk. Ripley's Museum of Rural Life at the bottom end of Robertsbridge has interesting specimens of iron-workings, cannons, old-style shops, a Victorian kitchen and a working forge.

REFRESHMENTS:

The White Horse Inn, Silver Hill.
The Seven Stars , Robertsbridge.
There are also other possibilities in Robertsbridge.

Walk 99   ASHDOWN FOREST EAST   10m (16km)

Maps: OS Sheets Landranger 188; Pathfinder 1248.

A walk on the eastern slopes of Ashdown Forest.

Start: At 514311, the car park in Croft Road, Crowborough.

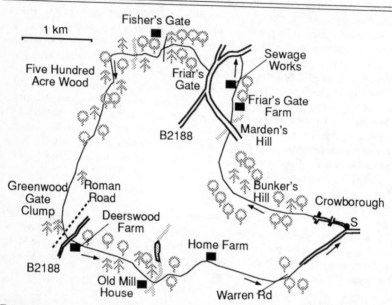

From the car park, walk to Crowborough Cross and then go westward along Beacon Road. Fork right into Beacon Gardens and, at the next junction, keep straight ahead along a tarmac drive to reach another junction. Turn right (still maintaining a westerly direction), cross a road and go down to a field. Now, go half-right towards posts flanking the entrance to a path through woods. Take the woodland path, going through the trees to emerge in open country with wonderful views across **Ashdown Forest** – to the west and north. The route continues ahead along the main forest ride of Bunker's Hill, maintaining height at first, but eventually dropping downhill, heading to the left of the houses at Marden's Hill. The path narrows as it approaches the road. Turn left along the road and then turn right into the access road to Friar's Gate Farm. About 50 yards along there is a 'Private Road' sign. Here, turn left on to a path. Go right over a footbridge, up some steps and then turn right to go alongside two fields. The route now joins a drive for a short distance, passing to the right of a paddock, then going left through a gate and alongside stables, to the right. Go down to a gate and stile in the bottom of a field. Go over and bear right on to a drive coming from the sewage works. Maintaining direction, northerly, continue to reach a lane. Turn left to reach the Half Moon Inn, and there turn left along the B2188. After 250 yards, turn right over a stile by a gate, on to a drive. Follow the drive to a fork, bearing left there. Walk past a house and then go right. A little further on, at a junction of paths keep on the main track, the Wealdway (*see* Note to Walk 72), going downhill to reach a stream. Cross the stream and ascend, with a fence on the right, to reach a fork. Keep to the right, following the Wealdway arrows, to go through a gate and up into Five Hundred Acre Wood, with its superb oak and beech trees. The Wealdway arrows reassure you on the walk through the trees. On emerging into open country, keep right along a sandy path ascending to Greenwood Gate Clump the highest point in the forest, about 720 feet (220 metres) above sea level. Keep the Clump to the right, continuing to cross the line of a **Roman Road**. Now fork right and walk to the B2188. Cross the road, with care – it can be busy, and follow the track ahead, passing to the left of Deerswood Farm. The path ahead is straightforward now, passing Old Mill House and Home Farm to join Warren Road. Turn left into Beacon Road and follow the signs back to the starting car park.

POINTS OF INTEREST:

Ashdown Forest– The forest is mainly open heathland and is an ideal walking area with over 80 miles of wide bridleways and 'rides' as well as many narrower footpaths through fields, heather, gorse, pines and deciduous trees. Fallow deer, badgers, grass snakes and, occasionally, adders are not uncommon companions for walkers.

Roman Road – More than a thousand years ago Ashdown Forest was noted as being 'impenetrable' yet Roman Roads have been located which appear to have joined *Londinium* to the South Coast via Greenwood Gate Clump, Camp Hill (close to the cluster of radio masts to the south), Isfield, and Barcombe and Malling Hill, Lewes. Today the Forest is a sandy heath covered with bracken, heather, gorse and many wild flowers. Five Hundred Acre Wood is probably the largest wooded area within it. The Forest Centre (at grid reference 432323) is full of relevant information and will add greatly to a visitor's enjoyment. Tel: 0342 823583.

REFRESHMENTS:

The Half Moon Inn, Friar's Gate.

There are also numerous possibilities in Crowborough.

Walk 100   CHIDDINGLY AND RIPE   12$^1/_2$m (19km)

Maps: OS Sheets Landranger 199; Pathfinder 1289.

Gently undulating farmland and quiet lanes, north of Eastbourne.

Start: At 544142, Chiddingly Church.

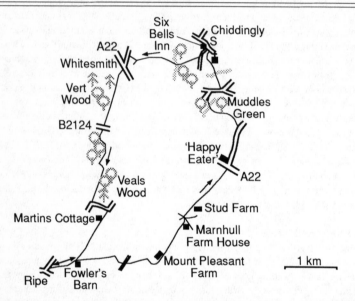

Take the lane leading south out of the village of **Chiddingly**, going past the Six Bells Inn, to the right, and the playing field, to the left. After 300 yards, turn right across a large field, heading towards a copse and a stream. Cross the stream by way of a footbridge and walk along the right edge of three fields to reach a lane by Whitesmith Farm. Turn left to a road junction. Now cross the A22 carefully and take the minor road going westward. Walk past the coniferous forest of Vert Wood, to the right, continuing to reach the B2124. Cross and go into the field opposite. Walk along its right edge to reach, after about 300 yards, a junction of paths. Go left and walk alongside a wood. When the wood ends, maintain direction for $^1/_2$ mile, soon skirting the right edge of Veals Wood and continuing to reach a lane at a bend. Turn left along the lane for about 350 yards, and when it turns sharp left enter the field on the right. Cross the field to the left corner and continue, walking to the left of Martin's Cottage. Now follow a bridleway past four fields to reach Fowler's Barn. Go diagonally right across three more fields to reach the village of **Ripe**.

After suitable refreshment and perhaps a stroll around the village, retrace your steps to Fowler's Barn and take the footpath heading right (due east) across three fields to reach a field corner. Turn right along the left edge of a field, then bear left across two more small fields to reach a road. Go right, and immediately left to enter a field just to the right of some buildings. Walk up to the top left corner, then go diagonally across the next field. Maintain direction across the next field corner, then go half-right (south-east) alongside two more fields to reach a major junction of paths and bridleways. Careful now! You need to go left along the main bridleway (north-eastwards), to walk to the right of Mount Pleasant Farm. Continue to reach the main A22 again.

Carefully cross (refreshments at The Happy Eater café) and walk along the lane opposite for $^3/_4$ mile (1 km) – look out for peacocks, to the right and perhaps owls too! – and, as the lane bears right at a small rise, take the footpath half-left and head due north. Continue alongside a copse, to the left, and cross a field to reach a hedge. Turn left and walk with the hedge for almost $^1/_2$ mile, descending to cross a stream then bearing right and up to emerge on to a lane. Turn right, and right again at a T-junction. This is Muddles Green. A further 250 yards brings you to a lane-fork: keep left and take the bridleway, to the left, just after passing a house. Keep to the left edge of a small conifer wood and soon descend, heading for the spire of Chiddingly Church. Maintain direction along the right edge of several fields to return to the churchyard and the start of the walk.

POINTS OF INTEREST:

Chiddingly – The church has a tall stone spire and, inside, a fine alabaster monument and a memorial to Mr and Mrs William Jefferay and their seven daughters.

Ripe – Do not miss the elegant and extravagantly carved private residence a few yards west of the Lamb Inn. The churchyard contains the grave of the poet and novelist Malcolm Lowry, the author of *Under the Volcano*.

REFRESHMENTS:

The Lamb Inn, Ripe.
The Six Bells Inn, Chiddingly.
The Happy Eater café, on the A22.

TITLES IN THE SERIES

Cheshire

County Durham

Derbyshire

East Sussex

Gloucestershire

Hampshire & the Isle of Wight

Lancashire

Northumberland

Somerset and Avon

Staffordshire

Surrey

Wiltshire

Yorkshire (Vols 1 and 2)